May Our Incense Rise

May Our Incense Rise

Jimmy L Wilcox

Xulon Press

Xulon Press
2301 Lucien Way #415
Maitland, FL 32751
407.339.4217
www.xulonpress.com

Contribution by Dan Melton, Colonel USMC

Cover Design - Xulon Press

Paperback ISBN-13: 978-1-6628-5010-3
Ebook ISBN-13: 978-1-6628-5011-0

Acknowledgements

First, I give thanks to my Lord and Savior, Jesus Christ, for giving me the ability and desire to write this book and for opening my understanding to the knowledge He wanted me to put in it. It was a challenging process and a journey I have never embarked on.

Thanks to my Uncle Raymond Riley who was always there as a mentor throughout my middle and high school years. You always took me with you to play basketball on the weekends and I was always welcomed in your house. I remember one Saturday afternoon as a teenager, you put a pen and a notepad in my hand and told me to start writing; that I could write poetry or anything I could imagine. Thank you, Uncle Ray, you inspired me to become a writer. I want to thank my friends, Ralph and Stephanie Washington, who came and picked me up almost every day when my wife passed away to just hang out with me, encourage me, and to make sure I didn't sink too low. Those were some difficult times for me and God lifted me by your friendship and by the prayers of many. Thank you for being my friends.

I want to thank my sons, Nicholas, Brandon, and Eric, for being a source of strength and encouragement for their father. I love you guys and I'm praying for each of you. I want to thank my sisters, Sharon Richardson, Renae Cartledge, and my mother, Rena Riley. In addition to the love and care you have always shown me, you guys were there two and three times a day, every day encouraging me both when my wife passed away and when I was down with Coronavirus until I fully recovered and was able to get back on my feet again. For that, my heart is still saying thank you with much love and gratitude for each one of you. Last but not least, I want to thank Evelyn Daniels for all the help you provided and for your editing suggestions. You have been a blessing to the brotherhood an inspiration to many. And to the many friends and family I did not mention, thank you so much.

Table of Contents

Chapter 1	*Nourishing the Presence of God*	1
Chapter 2	*Morning–Plow–Command Over Feelings*	7
Chapter 3	*The Freedom of Forgiving and Forgetting*	15
Chapter 4	*The Conditional Relationship*	21
Chapter 5	*Break Forth*	25
Chapter 6	*A Season and a Reason*	29
Chapter 7	*A Journey of Obedience*	33
Chapter 8	*The Stone That the Builders Rejected*	39
Chapter 9	*To Consider*	45
Chapter 10	*Finding Grace in His Sight*	48
Chapter 11	*Good Before Evil*	51
Chapter 12	*To Care For*	55
Chapter 13	*To Inquire*	59
Chapter 14	*To Admire*	64
Chapter 15	*To Seek*	76
Chapter 16	*This Poor Man Cried*	81
Chapter 17	*Inspect*	85
Chapter 18	*Making Mentions of You*	89
Chapter 19	*The Circle of Unity*	92
Chapter 20	*The Brand and the Name*	98
Chapter 21	*The Genesis and the Exodus of Time*	103
Chapter 22	*The Texture of Darkness*	105
Chapter 23	*To Be Darkened*	109

Introduction

Have you ever heard or used the phrase, reinvent the wheel? It's just modern terminology for doing an old thing better. We are always attempting to reinvent the wheel of time by doing things differently. And for the most part, we as the human race have succeeded in the efficacy of those endeavors. If we measured our progress from the beginning of time to where we are today, there is no doubt that the journey through time has yielded better results and conditions for the human race. The impact of those adjustments has given us the ability to enjoy life from a different point of view and a different standard of living than the generations of the past. But there was also another wheel that was reinvented about 2,000 years ago.

When Jesus Christ arose from the dead, He reinvented the wheel of the way life would be lived from that time forward by bringing in what is called a better covenant; a better way for the human race to have fellowship with their creator and new access into His holy presence. But even with a rebirth of a better way, it still doesn't shield us from the many challenges that life will present to us. The underlies, insecurity, and perplexities of our time are still forging their way into the hearts of mankind at such an alarming pace that people are checking out of this life without having made proper reservations for the life hereafter.

While we may be able to run and find some form of shelter from the falling rain, where can we run to for shelter when we are being rained on by the circumstances of life? It is for this reason I invite you to come along with me on this journey. Come along to experience a greater encounter of His reinventing the wheel of our desire and remaking us into the likeness of His very person. *May Our Incense Rise* is the heart's expression and desire for fellowship, with the creator of our existence, the one to whom we offer our incense. The scripture gives two distinct qualifications of a true worshiper. First, we must worship in spirit, and second, we must worship in truth.

> *But the hour cometh, and now is, when the true worshippers shall worship the Father in spirit and in truth: for the Father seeketh such to worship him. John 4:23*

The Father is seeking only after those who will allow Him to work in them a desire to be a true worshiper. A true worshiper is someone who does not discriminate on when to answer the call to worship, whether times are good or bad, sunshine or rain. A true worshiper gives God intentional worship regardless of the weather cast in their personal life.

> *For by him were all things created, that are in heaven, and that are in earth, visible and invisible, whether they be thorns, or dominions, or principalities, or powers: all things were created by him and for him. Colossians 1:16*

> *All things were made by him, and without him was not anything made that was made. John 1:3*

> *He is before all things, and by him all things consist. Colossians 1:17*

> *Thou art worthy, O Lord, to receive glory and honour and power: thou hast created all things and for thy pleasure they are and were created. Revelation 4:11*

God, through His infinite awareness of all things, designed and created us with a capacity and longing for worship. The individual will never feel complete until their capacity for worship has been satisfied. Since God's Word undeniably acknowledges Jesus Christ as the one who created all things, we must then consider Him as the instrument through whom our capacity for worship is fulfilled. The principle is that it has to first go through the Son before it can get to the Father. And because God has placed this principle within us, no creature will ever be complete until Jesus Christ becomes the object of their desire for worship. Nor will their worship be accepted before God unless it is channeled through Jesus Christ, the Son of God. Worship will then take on its truest and most profound meaning, through which we express the original purpose of our existence. It is through a daily devotion to God both morning and evening that our incense will rise as an odor of a sweet smell in the nostrils of God.

> *My voice shalt thou hear in the morning, O LORD; in the morning will I direct my prayer unto thee and will look up. Psalm 5:3*

> *Let my prayer be set before thee as incense, and the lifting up of my hands as the evening sacrifice. Psalm 141:2*

My prayer to God is that your eternal soul will be blessed by the words of this book. We were created to praise Him. We are created by Him and for Him and His pleasure. Our incense can only rise when we are aligned with the true purpose of our existence.

An English evangelist name Leonard Ravenhill once said, "The opportunity of a lifetime needs to be seized during the lifetime of the opportunity." Every day we are given a twenty-four-hour lifetime opportunity to offer up our incense to God, but we must take advantage of it in the morning and evening of that twenty-four-hour window of opportunity. This book is designed to help bring greater awareness and awakening to a personal relationship with Jesus Christ, to stimulate a desire in you, to put on your overcoming garments, and to get ready for the Lord's soon return. This will be the culmination of events, the one that we were spiritually born to live for. And now all things seem to imply that we are living in the season of that event. Just because you know that there will be a rapture doesn't mean the conviction of that knowledge is alive within you.

The world we once knew has changed before our eyes, and we can't go back to the way it was. We must develop a new paradigm for human mentality to meet the new era of human reality. So let us give credence to the eternal vigilance of the grace of God that caught our falling souls and rescued us into an everlasting hope of eternal life in Jesus Christ, so that we may be prepared for that glorious day, the catching away of the overcoming saints of God.

Prologue

I am so grateful that you have decided to come along with me on this journey. While there remains a little time before the coming of the Lord, we must be swift to identify the enemies that eat away at our time in both our individual and collective lives. We must qualify the events of our lives and those with who we choose to spend the greater portion of our time as either friends or enemies. Not that you are counting them as enemies, in a bad sense, but they could be enemies of your time, especially if your focus and values are different. Time is the greatest asset given to us and we can either buy it or sell it. We buy it with a continual, consistent ongoing relationship with Jesus Christ and we sell it by locking Jesus out of our choices and decisions, which will have no eternal value. Therefore, we should monitor our relationships to know the gravity and extent of the impact they have on us because our life is very brief and time sensitive.

The call to worship is an eternal call with eternal consequences, by either our obedience or disobedience to embrace the fellowship of the call. Who we spend the most of our time with will have the most influence on shaping our character. Character tells everyone who we are and who we are not. You cannot display qualities you never spent any time developing, and you can't withdraw what you haven't deposited. I can't display a moral character that I have never qualified through the medium of experience. There will be no reference to refer to those distinctive qualities, simply because I never considered them necessary for qualifying my behavior. It doesn't matter what kind of uniform you wear, or your position in life. You are who you are from the inside out, not from the outside in. The uniform an individual wear on the outside is not always a true reflection of who they are on the inside. Even Satan comes as an angel of light and false prophets as wolves dressed in sheep's clothing, those who are playing a role that contradict their true character.

> *Ye are our epistles written in our hearts, known and read of all men.*
> *2 Corinthians 3:2*

God wants to transform our lives into an epistle of Godly character and disposition. We are like a book with a cover page. Typically, the cover page of a book runs congruent with the contents inside of the book. We often say you can't judge a book by its cover and that is true, but you can judge a book by its content. The image we like to project to others and how we want to be perceived by them is our cover page. Our thoughts, feelings, and actions are the contents inside of our book. Are the contents inside of your book a true reflection of what's on the cover? Or do you have a different cover page for different groups of people because the content inside your book has no true identity? When you are at work you have one cover, and when you are at home you have another cover, but when you go to church, you display a different cover page than you do at home and work.

Are there noticeable variations in what you say and what you do? Especially when you are around certain people you want to impress or fit in with. If so, then what is on your cover page does not match the contents inside of the book, the walk and the talk are going in two different directions. This kind of book is very hard to read because it discriminates against continuity. But it doesn't have to stay that way if you desire that the contents in your book flow congruently with what is on the cover page. Then you no longer have to go around trying to project an outward image that you know you are not living up to. You must first align yourself with a more excellent paradigm and give a pledge of allegiance to not my will, but thine be done.

The only way to be a true worshiper is that the cover page and the contents of the book must bear the same image and be governed by the same standards of behavior. And as He summons us to the call of worship, may the sacrifice of our obedience arise as smoke along with the odor of our incense, as it ascends to God as, "...an odor of a sweet smell, a sacrifice acceptable and well-pleasing to God" (Phil. 4:18). We can do this together. Let the journey begin and *May Our Incense Rise*.

CHAPTER 1

Nourishing the Presence of God

Since the central focus of the message we want to convey through this book is concerning the rise of incense, which is a picture of our prayer life of worship and adoration to God and the Lamb, it will be helpful if we understand, to some degree, the necessary ingredients for making the incense along with its original meaning and the intended purpose. We will also visit some meanings of the word's *morning* and *evening,* since they are connected with the times the incense was to be offered, along with other meanings that I believe will help light the flame of desire to embark on a journey of offering our incense. The Hebrew meaning for the word incense is fumigation, a sweet perfume, the idea of fumigation in a close area (thus driving out the occupants), to smoke out, to turn into a fragrance by fire (as an act of worship), to sacrifice upon an altar of incense, just to name a few. Fumigation is the process of purifying and disinfecting. We may be able to observe through the range of meanings connected with the word incense, the strength of its capacity, and the reach of its influence.

The sweet incense consisted of five specific ingredients: stacte, onycha, galbanum, and frankincense and was tempered with salt. It was offered along with the morning and evening sacrifices. The incense was prepared by one called the apothecary, who measured and weighed the ingredients that were to be equal in weight. It was then delivered to the priest who performed the service in the tabernacle. And there were to be no other ingredients found like it throughout the entire nation.

> *And as for the perfume which thou shalt make, ye shall not make to yourselves according to the composition thereof: it shall be unto thee holy for the LORD. Whosoever shall make like unto that, to smell thereto, shall even be cut off from his people. Exodus 37-38*

The first meaning for *incense* is *to fumigate* in a close area and to thus drive out the occupants. It was through a continual offering of the incense both morning and evening that nourished God's presence among the tribes of Israel to give them strength to drive out the occupants of Canaan land. God's presence fumigated the land from idol worship and drove out the occupants. God told Moses:

> *Little by little will I drive them out before thee. Exodus 23:30*

Little by little, He conforms us into His image by driving out our bad attitudes and dispositions, the occupants of our flesh, while He shows us new mercies and compassion every morning. "Great is thy faithfulness unto us O God our Father." He doesn't expect us to change and be just like Jesus all at once.

Little by little, He works in us and through us, defining and developing those Christ-like qualities that He will present to Himself when we appear before Him. Look at the contrast between Christ and us and how we have so little tolerance with people, that we demand immediate change, or we want to drive them out of our presence, because we are not content with the little by little process. We take their need to change more personally than we take our own need to change, go figure. The truth is, if we don't accept the little by little process of change, neither will we accept an overnight change simply because the change is happening to someone else instead of us. Until change happens within us, we will not have enough tolerance to see it happen in someone else.

Incense also means to turn into a fragrance by fire as an act of worship. Sometimes God has to use the fire of afflictions to get us to offer our incense through an act of obedience. Afflictions are a form of suffering that He places us in to get us to do what we already know to do. God orders the fires of afflictions when He cannot get our attention any other way. He always uses afflictions as a last resort to rescue us from our own will and way. He doesn't allow the instrument of affliction to stay any longer than necessary. Once He begins to smell the fragrance of our worship again, the mission has been accomplished.

As long as Israel burned incense morning and evening and nourished God's presence, there was not an enemy who could defeat them. There wasn't a nation that was able to stand against them in battle because they nourished the presence of God in their midst. The more we nourish God's presence within us, the more faithful we will be to offer our incense. The burning of the incense was given by God as a command to Moses and Aaron for a perpetual statute throughout their generation. The ministry of burning incense along with all the service of the tabernacle was given for the priest alone.

And now, because of the new covenant, we can burn incense because we are a royal priesthood and a chosen generation. We each have an obligation as priests to burn incense and to nourish God's presence in our lives. God had to fumigate, disinfect and purify Canaan land of its previous inhabitants, because of the stink and unclean odor of idol worship and burning of incense to idols that nourished the presence of idolatry. And He likewise takes us through the process of fumigation to purify and disinfect us from the strange incense that nourishes the presence of mean, ugly, and unkind attitudes that are like dead flies sending forth a stinky odor from the ointment of the apothecary.

> *Dead flies cause the ointment of the apothecary to send forth a stinking savour. Ecclesiastes 10:1*

The incense was to be offered both morning and evening throughout their generation, or their lifetime. Our worship of God is never supposed to stop. It is to be a continual offering of incense unto God both morning and evening, throughout the remainder of our lifetime. By offering up our incense we nourish and cherish God's presence in our lives, and we drive out all fleshly occupants that are rivals to the name of Jesus.

> *And Aaron shall burn thereon sweet incense every morning: when he dresseth the lamps, he shall burn incense there upon. Exodus 30:7*

> *And when Aaron lighteth the lamps at evening, he shall burn incense upon it, a perpetual incense before the LORD throughout your generation. Exodus 30:8*

If you are not used to spending time with God morning or evening, now will be a good time to start. You have nothing to lose. You will get out of it what you put into it. And if you do spend some time with God but not quite enough, and you know that the Lord has been trying to engage you in a deeper prayer experience, try morning and evening. It is an experience that God has assured us of continual victory over our inward and outward enemies. It won't be difficult at all once you are willing to make an adjustment to the commitment, but it will be worth it and you can do it.

The Word of God says to "prepare to meet thy God" and this is how we prepare, by a continual offering of our daily morning and evening sacrifices of prayer and worship. God would not have given us a command to prepare to meet Him without providing the help we need to make it happen. This command speaks to both the present and the future. How we take heed to it will determine the extent of our preparation. Every person will be summoned by the creator to receive His final judgment for the choices made during our lifetime, to receive either a favorable or an unfavorable verdict from the just judge.

The choices we make in time will become the vehicle that will drive us to our eternal destination. In the final judgment, God will only point your vehicle of choices in the direction of travel, be it eternal life with Him or eternal damnation. We cannot live any kind of lifestyle we want and then put a sign that says Christian at the end of that type of lifestyle and think God is going to justify us just because we have a sign that says we are a Christian attached to the rear of our lifestyle. Especially when our choices contradict the kind of life a Christian should live. Man can cancel almost all his appointments with each other, but there are two appointments he will not be able to cancel.

> *For it is appointed unto men once to die, but after this the judgment. Hebrews 9:27*

The first appointment is death; he cannot cancel his appointment with death, nor can he bargain his way out of it. After death, the next appointment is the judgment. Man will not be a fugitive or a no-show because there will be no place to run and hide. Death does not discriminate on race, size, age, or quality of life. All men are equal in the grave. It doesn't matter how much of this world's possessions one has, the sting of death is going to serve the rich the same cup as it served the poor beggar. And all will lie down and return to the same substance they were before they stood up. All men are equal in death and judgment.

From dust thou art and unto dust shalt thou return. Genesis 3:19

So whether we prepare to meet Him or not, He has purposed an appointed time for you, me, and every human being to stand before Him and give an account of our preparation, or the lack thereof; thus receiving a final verdict from the just judge of heaven and Earth. "Shall not the judge of all the earth do right?" Genesis 18:25

CHAPTER 2

Morning-Plow-Command Over Feelings

The first meaning of *morning* is to *plow*. Every morning our physical bodies experience an awakening to a new beginning. The beginning of the new day starts at the conscious awakening to the physical reality of sound and movement. If you are anything like me in the morning, you will just lay there for a few moments while you align your mental and emotional self with your physical body. And then from there, you must choose to put your hand to the plow and begin to offer your incense of praise and worship before your feet ever touch the floor. The onward progression of time forces us to make immediate decisions to either begin to offer up our incense of worship or to reminisce over what we think our day is going to be like. I will admit that I can sometimes be that pendulum that swings both ways. And when it comes to getting up early, it's never a question of whether I feel like it because most of the time, just like you, I don't either. Once we become a little more mature we learn how to operate on both the positive and the negative sides of our feelings.

When we have been on the journey long enough we learn how to put our hands to the plow without consideration of how we feel. God commanded the priest to offer incense every morning and evening, it was to be done regardless of how the priest felt because the command superseded their feelings. The more obedient we become to the command the less we will consider our feelings. We must continue in our relationship with the Lord until the call to worship is answered by the command and not by feelings. Operating out of feelings will keep us absent from many calls to worship, many prayer meetings, many solitary moments of Bible study, and many ordained church services with the saints of God, which we are commanded not to forsake.

It is important to know that putting your hands to the plow is about your relationship with Jesus Christ, not your ministry. Here's why, I can give up my ministry and still have a personal relationship with the Lord, but I cannot give up my relationship and still have a ministry for him. However, I do believe that ministry plays a major part in our relationship with the Lord. When the definition of who we are can no longer be defined by our relationship with the Lord we have become backslidden. Then we will hide behind our ministry as long as we can get away with it. Ministry will become the fig leaves we are hiding behind to cover the nakedness of our relationship.

A plow was used for breaking up the ground, turning over and cultivating the soil, and preparing it to receive seed. We must plow daily in the field of our relationship with the Lord because not all the ground is equally pliable. There are some areas where we conduct ourselves better than others. We all struggle with common issues but perhaps at different times. Can you imagine what it would be like if we all were struggling with anger at the same time. Although it seems we are rapidly approaching such a time, it would be utterly chaotic, and the earth would be an insane asylum. It would be a pandemic much deadlier than Covid-19.

> *No man having put his hand to the plough and looking back is fit for the kingdom. Luke 9:62*

In so many words, Jesus was saying you can't move forward and look back at the same time because you will be living a reckless life, not fit for the kingdom. You must maintain a presence of mind that there are things behind that you need to forget or it will impact how far you can reach ahead. The only way to look back is to lose your vision of what is before you and the only way to continue forward is to lose your vision of what is behind you, either way, there is a vision that will be lost. You are the only one who can choose which vision you will lose and which vision you will keep.

I can't think of an issue more relevant among Christians who lose their vision and look back than unforgiveness. I both know and have heard of people who have turned loose of the plow because of unforgiveness. They had an experience that left them bitter and angry and those emotions gave birth to unforgiveness. Maybe they were hurt by some wrong inflicted upon them by someone they trusted; or an issue between them and someone else that wasn't resolved with integrity, or infidelity in a relationship, whatever it was it left an unforgivable impact on them toward the perpetrators.

Unforgiveness is a dysfunctional relationship with reality and a burden too heavy for the soul to carry. It is like carrying your own taskmaster with you everywhere you go. You are causing self-inflicting punishment when you hold on to unforgiveness. I am by no means minimizing the impact that the experience had on their lives because some people have been so hurt and torn by what someone else has done to them it is too difficult for them to talk about. Not only do they struggle with a painful memory but also with the emotions associated with the memory. The pain and the emotional trauma, the hurt, and loneliness of their experience, while hiding behind the dark shadows of silent resignation, and the screams from an inner prison that continue to fall on deaf ears of those who can't recognize the reality of their inner struggles, leave them pleading for answers to the question, "God why did you allow this happen to me?" This is a legitimate question when one doesn't know any other way of approaching God.

Some have been so abused mentally and emotionally that it is virtually impossible for any human being to reach that far inside of another regardless of how genuine the intentions may be. God alone knows the anguish of their hearts and the intensity of their struggle; all alone behind the prison doors of unforgiveness, beaten constantly by the taskmaster of their memory, forcing them to relive the stigma of past experiences, just to get a tighter grip on their eternal soul. Only the light of Jesus Christ and the medicinal qualities of the Word of God are capable of reaching that far into the darkness to extend to them an invitation to come forth from their mental and emotional dungeon, and remove the grave clothes of unforgiveness and adorn them with a robe of freedom.

> *As unto a light that shineth into a dark place, until the day dawn and the day star arise in your heart. 2 Peter 1:19*

Jesus Christ, the day star, shines in dark places regardless of how far the light has to travel to save the soul of mankind. It will penetrate through all dark places whether they are dungeons, caves, prisons, or graves, His light will seek, find and deliver you out of your darkness, into a new light. God can reach you wherever you are if you will just be honest enough to tell Him what is going on inside of you. Ask Him to help you forgive because you can't do it by yourself.

I can tell you about my own experience where I had unforgiveness toward a person well over a year, and the more I saw them the more I disliked them, I hated them. It made me feel good to know that they knew I hated them. At some point, I began to take heed to the convictions of the Spirit of God and the word that said if I don't forgive I will not be forgiven.

It affected my prayer life because I knew that I could not ask God to forgive me for anything until I had forgiven them. So I began to tell God exactly how I felt about the person. And I said, God, I hate them with so many different kinds of passion, and I can't stand to be around them and if I could get away with it, I would kill them.

You might say that is being too hateful and going a bit too far. But God already knew I felt that way toward that person. He just wanted me to be honest enough to confess what was going on inside of me. That is how I was taught to confess my sins no matter what they were. God wanted me to confess with my mouth what was in my heart so He could save me from it. And He wanted me to be real about my confession and not act super spiritual, because hate, anger, and unforgiveness are not fruits of the Spirit. I shared this with those readers who are honest and sincere enough to admit that they can identify and have identified with those same emotions inside toward someone who has hurt them.

Either you wished you could kill them or you did something to them and they wished they could kill you, Lol. We have to be honest because it goes both ways sometimes. We are not always the ones on the receiving end of the wrong. If truth be told, sometimes we are the ones to blame, because we started the whole thing. We just don't like admitting it because it places us in a negative light. What we inherited from our fore-parents Adam and Eve is in all of us, and all God has to do to bring it out, is to order the right set of circumstances.

In many things we offend all. James 3:2

After I told God how I felt about that person I finally came to a breaking point. I told God that I knew I wasn't supposed to be like that and begged Him to please change my heart and help me to forgive because I couldn't do it on my own. And He did. I asked God to renew a right spirit within me toward them, and He did that too. A right spirit is a spirit that is free of unforgiveness. This is how we must confess to break free from the chains of unforgiveness. Until we are willing to deal with the reason the problem will never be solved. We must see the bigger picture of the effects of unforgiveness. And we cannot see the picture as long as we are living in the frame. Unforgiveness is part of the frame. It doesn't matter how justified we feel about it, to forgive is a divine order and there are consequences if we don't. Just because we exclude ourselves from the narrative, doesn't mean God has excluded us and that we will not face the consequences of our exclusion.

And they forsook all to follow Jesus. Luke 5:11

One of the meanings for the word *forsook* is *to forgive*. No matter how much it may hurt, we cannot choose what we are going to forgive and what we are not going to forgive. If we want to be a true follower of Jesus, we must forgive everything. Jesus didn't die for some of our sins; He died for all of our sins. So we have to forgive everything if we are going to be a true follower of Jesus. When Jesus hung on the cross, He displayed a right spirit toward those who put Him there by crying out to the Father to forgive them. He didn't attempt to come down and avenge Himself for the wrong; He stayed there until it was finished.

There will be times when God will allow you and me to hang on the cross of circumstances and situations that He has purposed for us to go through. While we are hanging there, some will mock, some will scorn, ridicule, and belittle us, even laugh at us, just like they did Jesus. But the test will be to not allow what anyone says to cause us to come down from our cross. Regardless of how wrong we are treated, we have to hang there in that situation until God says "it is finished." Only then will we experience the resurrection of a new day. Sometimes the crosses we hang on before others are of our own making. We don't always act like Jesus when we are being mistreated or mishandled physically or verbally because we tend to associate how someone treats us with winning and losing. Since we don't like to lose, we strike back to defend our rights. No one is going to treat me like that and get away with it, is what we say. How do I know? Been there, done that too. To forgive and to ask for forgiveness when we have wronged others is how we win the right way.

> *He is bought as a lamb to the slaughter, as a sheep before her shearers is dumb, so he openeth not his mouth. Isaiah* 53:7

This is the prophecy of Jesus Christ when He would go before the judgment of the chief priest and Pontius Pilate, the procurator, to be condemned to die. Yet in His unfair trial, He was blameless and harmless and forgiving to His offenders. I believe the example Jesus was teaching us was that some major victories are only won through silence. You should purpose in your heart not to give sleep to your eyes until you lift your hands toward heaven and ask God to help you forgive everybody for everything they've done that has brought hurt, pain, and injury to your life; even if you don't feel like it, do it anyway. Remember this is about command over feelings. What God has commanded us to do supersedes how we feel about doing it.

Don't get angry if the person you forgive doesn't change. When you forgive someone for a wrong it changes you, not the person you forgave. They may not ever choose to change, or they may have already changed before you ever forgave them. People do change for the better, but unforgiveness will never give them a chance to prove themselves. God will not forgive us for anything until we have forgiven others for everything. If you meant what you said, He will work His forgiveness in you and through you, just as He has done for untold millions.

> *For it is God who worketh in you both to will and to do of his good pleasure. Philippians 2:13*

CHAPTER 3

The Freedom of Forgiving and Forgetting

Although we have already touched on unforgiveness in the previous segment, because of how big the subject is, we will only mention a few things more, but from a different perspective. When we forgive and when we receive forgiveness, it removes heavy burdens from our souls and unlocks prison doors. It allows the bells of freedom to ring from the corridors of our imagination to the dungeons of silent resignation. As the song says, "When the shadows of this life are gone, I'll fly away." Unforgiveness is one of the shadows of this life and the only way to fly away from it is to forgive. When we don't forgive, we lock ourselves up for a wrong that was committed against us by someone else.

Once you forgive you release yourself and you feel "like a bird, from prison bars have flown." And you will be able to fly away from the dungeon of despair to reclaim the hope of your calling. Out of your bondage and into new freedom. Some feel they cannot move forward in life until they hear the person they have committed an offense against say to them, I forgive you. That may not ever happen. However, you must ask for forgiveness from the one you have offended, preferably face to face, if it can be arranged. This provides the opportunity for them to see and hear the sincerity of your confession. (I am very sorry for what I said and how I said it and for what

I've done. I take full responsibility for my wrong actions that offended you. Will you please forgive me? And if we are going to have a friendship or relationship to any degree in the future, can we begin to build it today from the foundation of my request for your forgiveness.)

If they don't want to hear your voice or see your face there is nothing you can do about that. You have to go to God and present your cause to Him and once He sees and hears your sincere confession and repentance for the offense, He will exonerate you regardless if the other person ever does. From that time forward, you have to learn how to get above the cause and the effects of what people think about you, so you can live in the free existence of your new reality. Sometimes people will say, I will forgive, but I won't forget. What they are saying is that I am going to let you feel free but I am going to keep the memory of what you did in prison. The reality is, you're not truly free because if the memory of what you did is in prison, then so are you.

> *It is for freedom that Christ has set us free, therefore keep standing firm and do not be subject again to a yoke of bondage. Galatians 5:1*

Once you take your case before the Lord and He forgives you, even when the individual hasn't and will not forgive you, this is where you have to learn to defend your forgiveness from heaven's point of view. When God forgives, He also forgets the wrong we have done and records it in the archives of heaven, which will reflect that your offense has been forgiven and forgotten. This is the record you must defend if you are going to remain free. Do not accept any other record or you will subject yourself again to a yoke of bondage. Fight for the forgiveness that God gave you and because God has forgotten, you have to forget, in a sense that the memory of it no longer has the power to control you mentality or emotionally. When someone tries to remind you about your past fault or failure, you have to defend what has been recorded in heaven by whatever means possible.

Let no one put back on you a guilt image that God has taken off of you and has delivered you from, no matter what it was, or who it is, simply do not accept accusations of your past failures. You must tell them respectfully (ma'am or sir) I'm sorry, but I do not drink reclaimed water. They will understand what you mean. Your freedom also depends on you assuming the responsibility of living a morally clean life and not repeating the same offenses over again.

> *When Jesus had lifted up himself, and saw none but the woman, he said unto her, Woman, where are those thine accusers? Hath no man condemned thee? She said, No man, Lord. And Jesus said unto her, Neither do I condemn thee; go and sin no more. John 8:10-11*

Jesus, the living Word, justified the woman on the spot with the kind of forgiveness that superseded their condemnation of her. And for her to fully enjoy the freedom given to her, He commanded her to go and sin no more. Now you have a responsibility to share this same kind of freedom with those who have offended you, and never say I will forgive, but I won't forget. That's a mockery of the grace of God that He has freely given to you. And it's not that you forget what a person did to you, it's that you don't remember with a desire for revenge or retaliation against the one who committed the offense. You are free from a revengeful, retaliatory attitude, and disposition against the offender.

And when he had begun to reckon, one was brought unto him, which owed him ten thousand talents. But forasmuch as he had not to pay, his lord commanded him to be sold, and his wife, and children, and all that he had, and payment to be made. The servant therefore fell down, and worshiped him, saying, Lord, have patience with me, and I will pay thee all. Then the lord of that servant was moved with compassion, and loosed him, and forgave him the debt. But the same servant went out, and found one of his fellow servants, which owed him a hundred pence: and he laid hands on him, and took him by the throat, saying, Pay me that thou owest. And his fellow servant fell down at his feet, and besought him, saying, Have patience with me, and I will pay thee all. And he would not: but went and cast him into prison, till he should pay the debt.... Then his lord, after that he had called him, said unto him, O thou wicked servant, I forgave thee all that debt, because thou desirest me Shoudest not thou also have had compassion on thy fellow servant, even as I had pity on thee. Matthew 18:24-29

Those of you who are familiar with this parable know that it is about giving the same kind of mercy to others that you have received from God. God will not tolerate us asking Him for forgiveness for our offenses and then we refuse to forgive the offense of others. The wicked servant presented a false narrative and a fictitious representation of how God wants us to express His forgiveness toward each other. He was forgiven ten thousand talents worth of debt which equated to 200,000 years of labor, 60,000,000 days of work, and 3.48 billion dollars in debt. Yet, he would not show the same kind of compassion on someone who only owed him 11,733 dollars. What a price to pay for holding on to unforgiveness.

On the Day of Atonement, there were two goats brought before the Lord by the high priest for the nation of Israel. One goat was the Lord's goat, and the other goat was called the scapegoat. The high priest would kill the Lord's goat at the brazen altar before the Lord. This represented forgiveness. The high priest would then lay His hands upon the scapegoat and confess all the sins of the nation of Israel and then choose a fit man to carry the goat away into the wilderness, or a place uninhabited. The goat is said to have fallen or was pushed over a cliff to its death. The scapegoat represented the forgetfulness of sins. The picture of the two goats represents the unified connection of unbroken fellowship between forgiving and forgetting. John the Baptist hailed Jesus as the Lamb of God.

> *Behold the Lamb of God which taketh away the sins of the world. John 1:20.*

This verse represents both goats in one body. The Lamb of God who was crucified and shed His blood on cavalry before the Lord was for the forgiveness of sins. This is why when Jesus died on the cross He said, "Father forgive them, for they know not what they do." "Which taketh away the sins of the world" represents the scapegoat for forgetfulness of sins.

The scapegoat could not take away the sins of the world until after the Lord's goat had been sacrificed. The sins of the world could not be taken away until the death of the Lamb of God. When Jesus arose from the dead, He arose as the perfect High Priest who went and applied the blood on the mercy seat in heaven, one time for all time. The blood of the scapegoat represents a river of remission that carries our sins away to never be remembered again, into the sea forgetfulness behind the back of God.

Behold for peace I had great bitterness but thou hast in love to my soul delivered it from the pit of corruption: for thou hast cast all my sins behind thy back. Isaiah 38:17

He will return again, he will have compassion on us; he will subdue our iniquities; and thou will cast all their sins into the depths of the sea. Micah 7:19

These two verses let us know that there is a sea behind the back of God where our sins are cast to be remembered no more. Our confidence is that when we ask for forgiveness of sins, the sin is not only forgiven but forgotten at the same time. The only reason that is possible is that the Lord's goat and the scapegoat have been eternally joined together as the "forgiver and the forgetter" of sin in the same body. He is both goats in one body and because of that, He cannot tell us He will forgive our sins but He won't forget them as this would be a contradiction in His very person.

You can't say I forgive but I won't forget because the principle says that you cannot have one without freely giving the other, they are inseparable. We must continue on our journey with the Lord until the nature of both goats is joined together and formed within us. The perfect spotless Lamb of God (the Lord's goat), the perfect scapegoat, and the perfect High Priest all joined together in one body have brought complete perfection to the atonement.

And not only so, but we also joy in God through our Lord Jesus Christ, by whom we have now received the atonement. Romans 5:11

CHAPTER 4

The Conditional Relationship

Perhaps to some degree, the shoe fits us all, especially when God opens our eyes and lets us see how conditional we are. Some Christians think they have cut some kind of deal with God that their obedience to Him must be based on God doing something for them in return. They want a relationship with God and offer to serve only if the conditions are right for them. Their walk with Christ is only as good as the conditions that surround them and when their conditions change their walk changes.

When we allow certain conditions to dictate our fellowship with the Lord, it's because we are partial and God is only good as long as He is blessing us with good things, good feelings, and good vibrations. Freedom from any difficulty or adversity is what we call the good life.

The children of Israel left Egypt for the good life in a land flowing with milk and honey. They witnessed how good God had been amid all the plagues He sent upon the Egyptians and He spared them in the midst of it all. With the Passover blood over the lintel and the two side posts of the door, they were spared from the death angel that destroyed all the firstborns of the Egyptians. They saw God divide the waters and make a pathway for them to walk on dry ground amid the sea, and they saw God drown the armies of the Egyptians, causing the waters to return to its strength. And when they beheld all these great and mighty miracles that God had done they held their first church service on the other side of the sea. They sang, they shouted, they danced, you name it, they did it. They expressed their gratitude to God for what He had done in their present condition.

They had no problem with how God was running the show as long as the conditions looked right and felt right to them. Little did they know that their journey had only just begun. The very first test that God allowed them to go through was at Marah where the waters were bitter. Conditions had changed and their approval rating of how God was running the show had fallen into the unfavorable category just that soon. They did not welcome the difficulties that God was using to test and try them. Their attitude on display toward God was as bitter as the waters that He had brought them to.

Sometimes God brings us to bitter situations on the outside to show us how bitter we are toward Him on the inside about the way He is directing our lives. Our fluctuating opinion of God doesn't change who He is nor does it negate His position of authority to rule over the affairs of our lives and to order it however He pleases. The scriptures never record where they asked God to forgive them for their bitter attitude against Him at Marah. And we know they did not repent by how often they continued to showcase their disapproval of God and His servants throughout their wilderness journey. When God had enough with that generation, He pronounced a final verdict that prevented them from possessing the land He had planned for them to obtain. We must ask God to forgive us for the many bad attitudes and dispositions that we have displayed toward Him while on this Christian journey.

All because conditions were not in our favor and things didn't work out the way we wanted them to doesn't mean that we can murmur and complain against God without eventually suffering the consequences. Israel could not enjoy the journey they were on because they were too focused on how things were in Egypt. They began to miss the onions, leeks, and garlic because they were more focused on where they came from than where God was taking them to. Just like Lot's wife, it wasn't that she turned her head and looked back, but she looked back in her heart first, because she had an inner connection to the things she had to leave behind. What we value the most in our hearts will eventually turn our heads in that direction.

This is why when some people get saved they only hold on for just a short time before they return to their former surroundings, their former comfort zones. They somehow feel that God is taking more from them than He is giving to them. Their inner connection with the world would not allow them to believe that God was able to give them something better than what they left behind. They consider the things the scriptures say that as Christians they should not do weightier than the things the scriptures say they can do for Christ. They don't give the grace of God enough margins to work in them and on their behalf, because they don't place enough value on having a relationship without conditions. So not long after they start, they look back to the things of this world and turn loose of the plow.

They are like the character Pliable in the book *Pilgrim's Progress*. Pliable started soon after he heard Pilgrim's testimony about the Celestial City. It all sounded good enough for him to follow along. They set forth on their quest to the celestial city and he had a good talk until they came to a place called the Slew of Despondency, where he met with conditions that he didn't expect to encounter. The writer went on to say that Pliable got out of the Slew of Despondency on the side close to his own house. He turned back to familiar territory and familiar surroundings which were on the side close to his own house. But Pilgrim continued alone on his journey to the celestial city.

Many start on the journey and look very promising but when faced with unexpected testing and trials they get out of the race on the side closest to their own house of habits. Even now, many Christians are giving up their testimony of being faithful witnesses for Christ because they are being lured away by the temporal attractions of the world's delusions and falsehoods. They become disenchanted with how God orchestrates and presides over the affairs of their lives.

God will sometimes disrupt the ebb and flow of the things we are connected with to allow us to see how much value we have placed on those things compared to our relationship with Him. One songwriter coined the phrase, "You can take the dearest things from me if that's how it must be, for me to draw closer to you Lord." God expects us to give Him thanks even when we don't understand what He is doing and why He is doing it. Our motivation for serving God should always be relationship-driven, not condition-oriented. If it isn't, we will become disappointed when things don't go the way we want them to go. Giving thanks doesn't mean that it will always be easy to accept but it does establish the principle of what we should do regardless of how difficult it may be. When our response is to Him instead of to the circumstances that He places us in, then the incense of our worship will ascend to Him regardless of how favorable or unfavorable the conditions may be.

CHAPTER 5

Break Forth

Morning also means to break forth, which means *to break out in a joyful sound and to make a loud noise.* Just as the early rays of the sun break forth through the long night to the joyful sound of the vibration of creation, so also our morning worship is the early rays of our joyful sound of love and obedience to the Lord's command. Intentional worship is the first fruit of our day that we offer up to God through love and obedience. The first fruits were brought into the house of the Lord and given unto the priest; this was their portion of the harvest for their sacrifice and service to the whole nation of Israel.

Jesus Christ was made a High Priest forever after the order of Melchizedek. And because He is our eternal High Priest we are to offer up our worship as first fruits to Him for making the ultimate sacrifice and service for the entire human race on the cross at Mount Calvary. Sometimes, because of the longevity of the night season, we may want to question God as to how long before daybreak? How long will I have to go through this? The answer is, as long as it's needed, yet not one second more than necessary. It is in these dark seasons that He works godly character within us. Growth takes place in the night seasons, the most challenging times of our walk with Christ. We have to hold on until the early rays of His grace and mercy come shining through our dark sky to rescue us from the shadows of a long, dark, and difficult night of testing and trials. To make it through our night seasons we have to remain connected through our praise and worship and don't allow the darkness to dictate our actions. This will become the well you can drink from and a reservoir of choices that will not allow you to abandon your relationship with Jesus Christ.

> *Weeping may endure but for a night, but joy cometh in the morning. Psalm 30:5*

And when the early rays of the joyful sound of the day season begin to shine through then you will sing a new song and your hope will be renewed for the Journey ahead. When Jesus, the Son of Righteousness, called Lazarus to come forth from the dead, Lazarus experienced the early rays of resurrection power.

> *And when he thus had spoken, he cried with a loud voice, Lazarus, come forth. And he that was dead came forth, bound hand and foot with grave clothes: and his face was bound about with a napkin. Jesus saith unto them, loose him, and let him go. John 11:43-44*

There must have been something very special about Lazarus because Jesus often resided there when He was in Bethany. Before he died, his sisters sent messages to Jesus begging Him to come and heal him saying he whom thou lovest is sick. Jesus purposely tarried because He knew the miracle His Father wanted to perform. Once He arrived at the grave, Lazarus had already been dead for four days. He ordered them to roll the stone away from the tomb and then cried with a loud voice, "Lazarus, come forth!" And he who was dead came forth from the tomb. Just like Lazarus, you are someone who Jesus loves. Jesus loves you just as much as He loved Lazarus and there is something inside of you that He wants to call forth and bring back to life again. Oh yeah, you still go to church, and you still sing along during worship service, but how often is Jesus at your house after church is over like he was at Lazarus' house? How often do you spend time in fellowship with the Lord outside of the walls of church? What kind of conversations are you having when you are away from the saints and what kind of people are you entertaining?

Jesus was always residing at Lazarus, Mary, and Martha's house whenever He was in Bethany. Do you make time for Jesus outside of church attendance? Jesus wants to resurrect your first love that will always have time for Him. You have to learn how to let the Christ in you make a loud noise for your first love relationship to come forth like it used to be when Jesus was the center of all of your decisions for friendships and fellowship.

The new man inside of you needs to scream and make a loud noise sometimes and when you give Him the freedom to do so, you will see things coming alive on the inside that have been lying dormant for a while. You will experience an awakening to a new vision of Jesus and to the kind of relationship He wants to have with you. Once you learn the secret of screaming and crying out with a loud voice as Jesus did at the tomb of Lazarus, you will live again.

The devil knows the power of noise, that is why he tries to keep loud praises out of the church because the louder the praise, the more power. The more power, the more victory, and freedom people will experience when they understand and are not ashamed of it. If you want to experience a new freedom, start making a loud noise unto God sometimes and see what happens. If you are too embarrassed to do it in front of people, and your church doesn't believe in praising God with a loud voice, get in your car and go for a ride and let it rip. Just do it. You must understand that there are some things you can call back to life again and into new freedom that comes from loud praises. This prophetic psalm tells of how Jesus cried when He was in death and hell, for His Father to come and rescue Him.

> *In my distress I called upon the LORD, and cried unto my God: he heard my voice out of his temple, and my cry came before him, even into his ears. Psalm 18:6*

The word for cried is to call loudly, to shout, and to yell. So we see even Jesus practice making a loud noise unto the Father to come and get Him out of death and hell after He had fulfilled all of God's purpose and plan to redeem mankind. And the loud noise that He made when He cried to His Father allowed Him to experience the freedom of resurrection by the glory of the Father. After three days, Jesus experienced the breaking forth of the early rays of resurrection morning from the night season in death and hell for you and me. And now that he is risen from the dead, there is a love song he sings from the cross to the souls of the human race. The song says "I love you, I love you, that's what Calvary said. I love you, I love you, I love you, written in red." He wrote I love you to the human race with his own blood.

CHAPTER 6

A Season and a Reason

In different ways and for different reasons, at different times and in different seasons, God orders the events of our lives. And as the seasons take their turn there are lessons we must learn. In learning, we must become pliable enough to yield to the process that introduces us to a challenge of a greater walk with Christ, through the medium of sometimes painful and difficult circumstances. Pain and difficulty are sometimes necessary instruments for the potter's hand to fashion us into the vessel that He desires us to become. The character we develop and the person we become in the process will be far more valuable than anything tangible we achieve through the outcome. When we learn how to cooperate with how God is working in our lives, we will stop asking Him *why*. Our biggest question is always *why?* We somehow feel that God is not being fair with us when He doesn't tell us why we are going through some circumstances, and because that question isn't answered yet, our fellowship with God goes into standby. So now, because *why* has become the obstruction in our vision we no longer give God our intentional praise and worship.

We struggle through our offering to find the cohesiveness to keep our commitments in place when we don't understand why God is allowing certain things to happen to us. When *why* becomes the obstruction, your vision will become so dim that you won't be able to see past yourself. *Why* is a thief and robber that will never allow you to worship God with your whole heart in the hard and difficult times, especially when you are the one who is directly affected by the *why*. When we can't be the narrator of our experiences with God, we compare fantasy to reality, how we want it to be to how it is; what we wish we had to what we actually have. God will not leave us in a situation any longer than He has appointed for us to be there if we do not rebel against Him. Rebellion against God can prolong our stay in situations where He would have already taken us out of it.

It was not God's will for the children of Israel to wander forty years in the wilderness. Their wandering was based totally upon how they responded to the things that God allowed them to go through. By their constant murmuring and complaining they became enemies of God's will, His purpose, and plan for their present and future existence. Constantly murmuring and complaining over how God is running the affairs of our lives can cause us to become an enemy of God's purpose for our present and future existence.

I have never seen it recorded in the scripture where they thanked God for the hard times He allowed them to go through; no gratitude to God for anything He had already done and no grateful call to remembrance of His goodness and mercy. Forgetfulness can be a great ally when it is attached to forgiveness, and it can also be one of our biggest enemies when we don't remember the goodness of God when we are going through hard times. We forget all the things that God has already done for us. Since those experiences are not our present reality, our inner enemies of murmuring and complaining strike out against God and begin to accuse Him of being unfair, unjust, and not giving us the best. Regardless of what happens on the outside, we are moved by what is compelling us from within. Although we do struggle from outward mentalities, our greatest enemy dwells within. Our actions and reactions come from what controls us from within.

For from within out of the heart of men proceed, Evil Thoughts, Adulteries, Fornications, Murders, Thefts, Covetousness, Wickedness, Deceit, Lasciviousness, an Evil Eye, Blasphemy, Pride and Foolishness: All these evil things come from within and defile the man. Mark 7:21-23

Jesus said all of these things live on the inside of us and these are the things that defile us in the eyes of God, not what happens on the outside. The descendants of Adam and Eve have all of these evil things on the inside and are capable of this kind of behavior. So because we have the same nature within us, someone's anger against us calls to the same anger inside of us and sometimes causes us to retaliate with the same words and actions. Whatever is not Christ-like have their origin and behavior in all of these evil things. These are our true lifetime enemies; they live on the inside of our fleshly house. The apostle Paul referred to the body as an earthly house for the soul and spirit.

For we know that if our earthly house is destroyed, we have a building from God, a house not made with hands, eternal in the heavens. 2 Corinthians 5:1

The time will come when a man's enemies will be members of his own house. Matthew 10:36

Now you can take that literally if you choose and it may have literal significance, but a spiritual awakening will cause one to look into a deeper aspect of it. The time will come for sincere Christians to take a deeper look at where their real enemies reside. The time will come when a man will be enlightened by the revelation that his real enemies are members from inside of his own temple. These lifelong enemies live inside of our earthly house and they travel with us everywhere we go. You don't have to be in a certain place to get angry, or to cuss or lust. These actions are common among men and prove that we all have the same inherited nature with the same capacity for wrong. I'm not promoting it; I'm just trying to enlighten your awareness of the propensity for this sort of activity that lives within us. The Truth is, **My real enemy is my inner me!**

The Lord has promised to deliver us from all enemies and to drive out the inhabitants. What He did for the children of Israel on the outside under the old covenant, He wants to do for you and me on the inside with a new and better covenant. Honest confession and repentance are the forerunners that give the blood of Jesus a triumphant entry into our temple to cleanse us from these evil members of our house. Remember, little by little will He drive out these enemies. Just as He told the children of Israel that He would drive out the inhabitants of the land, so also will He do the same for us.

> *I will call upon the LORD, who is worthy to be praised, so shall I be saved from my enemy. Psalm 18:3*

This is a song of David when God had delivered him from all his enemies, even Saul. Notice the first reason David called on the Lord. It wasn't to be saved from his enemies; it was because He is worthy to be praised. David set the order straight. There is nothing wrong with asking God to save us from our enemies, but we must understand exactly how God wants us to approach Him. He saves us from our enemies automatically when the order is straight and the conditions are right. When our reason for praising Him is rooted in our purpose for existing, then our enemies become God's enemies, because they are not fulfilling their purpose for existing. "If God be for us, who can be against us?" When they are against us, they are really against the one who is for us.

CHAPTER 7

A Journey of Obedience

When we consider the life of Abraham, we instantly associate it with the time when God commanded him to slay his son Isaac, the son of the promise. He was commanded to go into the land of Moriah and there, offer up Isaac as a sacrifice.

> *And he said, take now thy son, thy only son Isaac, whom thou lovest, and get thee into the land of Moriah; and offer him there for a burnt offering.* Genesis 22:2

If you don't think the enemy of feelings was riding shotgun with Abraham, you better think again. *Feelings are only our enemy when we allow them to become the reason why we don't obey God.* Do you think that Abraham was excited about slaying his son? Or do you think Abraham felt like obeying God on that occasion? Absolutely not! What man who loves his son wants to kill him? God was testing Abraham to see if he trusted God more than his feelings and for other reasons much bigger than that. There will be times as we journey on with God that He will present to us difficult challenges by placing us in situations that force us to make difficult choices because He desires to know by experience the degree of our loyalty and obedience to His Word.

Isaac means *laughter*, and on this occasion, Abraham had nothing to laugh about. It was the most difficult and inappropriate time for laughter. Yet, Abraham refused to accuse God of being unjust in the thing he was commanded to do. So Abraham set his face toward the land of Moriah to honor God's command. Regardless of the difficulty of the request God is asking of us, we must set our face like flint toward the command and from there, embark on a journey of obedience until we reach our destination. Abraham, Isaac, and a few servants of his household arose early to embark on a three-day journey to the land of Moriah. Rising early to offer up our incense to God through worship is how we prepare for our day's journey.

Abraham had plenty of time and opportunity to reflect on what God told him to do and could have turned around if that consideration was still on the table. He removed any consideration of turning back before he started on his journey. There must come a time in our walk with Christ that certain considerations and choices must be taken off the table. To do certain things, to go to certain places, and to hang with certain people are no longer options. They must be excluded from the list of choices we need to make to be obedient and faithful to the journey we have been called to go on.

When Abraham finally arrived in the land of Moriah, he said to his servants, "Abide here and I and the lad will go yonder and worship, and will come again to you." There are certain stops in our spiritual journey where we must leave behind both friends and family because it becomes a solitary walk of obedience from that time forward, without any outward influence. Abraham didn't know that it was just a test but still he was willing to obey God's command.

I believe that God has the sovereign right to challenge the stability of our commitments to Him by whatever means He deems necessary. Sometimes, the things He allows us to go through may seem more like a mess than a test. But if we channel the spirit of Abraham, the father of faith, we will be able to continue in the journey without being guided by our feelings. When they finally arrived at their destination, it tested Abraham's final obedience, which was to comply with the Lord's command. When God saw that Abraham would obey Him to the very end, the angel of the Lord cried out to Abraham not to harm his son, Isaac.

> *Abraham, Abraham.... Lay not thine hand upon the lad, neither do thou anything unto him: for now I know that thou fearest God, seeing thou hast not withheld thy son, thine only son from me. Genesis 22:11-12*

God saw Abraham's final obedience and was pleased with the outcome. Therefore, God provided a ram in the bush for Abraham to sacrifice instead of his son. God not only wants to know our initial obedience, but He wants an experience with our final obedience. God is a faithful keeper of His promise to those who are faithful keepers of His Word. How many rams have we left in the bush that God did not allow us to see because our final obedience did not join our initial obedience; therefore, the blessing that God would have given us has been given to someone else who met the conditions and passed the test?

When I look back through the years, I can see rams that I left in the bush because I never joined my final obedience to my initial obedience. It had gotten so bad that God once spoke to me while my wife and I were visiting my sister and her husband on the east coast of Florida. He said these words to me, "I want you to learn how to delight over the decisions that I delight to make for you." I guess God was fed up with the decisions I was making for myself, so He took over. I was always taught that God has good, better, and best. "And he gives the best to them who leave the choice to him" (Ps. 37:7). And God said to me, "If you do not pass the test, you cannot have the best." Now that Abraham had passed the test, he could laugh again because God provided a sacrifice in Isaac's place.

Just because we don't understand what God is doing, and we don't see the necessity of it, doesn't mean that we should start accusing God of being unfair. We must be very careful how we order our conversation about the way God is running the show even when we are totally in the dark on why things are going the way they are. We can still order the right conversation before God on how He desires to operate and orchestrate His plan for our lives.

> *Whoso offereth praise glorify me: and to him that ordereth his conversation aright will I show the salvation of God. Psalm 50:23*

There is a proper order in which we must speak to God in the hard times. These are truths that I have been taught over the years. We must first give thanks to God for everything just the way it is and then bless His name.

> *In everything give thanks for this is the will of God in Christ Jesus, concerning you. 1 Thessalonians 5:18*

Job is a great example of how to do that. He lost all of his children, all of his substance, his flocks, and his body was covered with boils. Yet, Job did not charge God foolishly. In so many words, Job ordered his conversation the right way. When you consider all that Job lost in one day, it would be an unbearable cross for you and me to carry. Thank God He chose Job as an example to us, of what to do with a much lighter cross to bear. Job recognized God's hand in it and that is why he said, "Naked came I from my mother's womb, and naked shall I return thither: The LORD gave and the LORD has taken away; blessed be the name of the LORD" (Job 1:21).

The second step is to acknowledge God as the head over your problem, and the one who allowed it to happen.

And hath put all things under his feet, and gave him to be the head over all things to the church. Ephesians 5:22

Stop blaming the devil for things that God is allowing you to go through because He wants you to give Him an experience of obedience to His Word regardless of how difficult it is. He wants an experience with your initial and final obedience. If you remember the story, God signed off on what happened to Job. The devil couldn't do anything until God approved it. It is an immature Christian who blames the devil for the hard times just because they refuse to accept the truth that a God who loves us so much is the same God who is allowing suffering to come into our world. The life of Job is proof that God wants us to be mature Christians and the only way He can perfect us is by sometimes placing us in painful positions and conditions to teach us lessons that we cannot learn any other way. Jesus was made perfect through suffering and if we are going to be conformed into His likeness, then we too must travel down the Via Dolorosa (the road of suffering).

For it became him, for whom are all things, and by whom are all things, in bringing many sons to glory, to make the captain of their salvation perfect through sufferings. Hebrews 2:10

And finally, we must humble ourselves and do not allow pride to win. I once heard a saying, "Pain will teach us lessons that our pride wouldn't let us learn." I can certainly agree with that statement. I had to go through years of pain to learn lessons that my pride wouldn't let me learn at the time I was supposed to learn them. It is easy to order our conversation right when everything is going according to plan but the test is when God allows the pain to come and the pleasure to cease. When nothing goes according to plan and it seems like you are going to be swallowed up by the whale of your circumstances, it's not so easy then. Having a better understanding of the nature of the journey you are on, and who is really in control, is how we will snatch victory from the jaws of defeat. This is the time and place where spiritual growth and moral development begin. This is where we give God an experience; it is the space between our initial and final obedience to His Word and command.

> *He that hath my commandments and keepeth them, he it is that loveth me, and he that loveth me shall be loved of my Father. John 14:21*

We prove our love to God through obedience to His Word and spirit, and by no other means or methods does He use to draw us into fellowship with Himself. If we love Jesus as much as we say we do, the only proof of our love that God will accept is obedience to His Word and His Spirit. As the song goes "Trust and obey, there's no other way to be happy in Jesus, but to trust and obey." While your Mount Moriah experience may not be to offer up your sons and daughters, whatever He is calling you on a journey of obedience to offer up, do not stop until your initial and final obedience has been accomplished. Only then will you be able to completely enjoy the blessing of whatever ram He has placed in the bush for you.

CHAPTER 8

The Stone That the Builders Rejected

The word for *stone* in Hebrew is *Eben,* which means to build and is traced back to a root word *Bane'* which means *a son as the builder of the family name, it means the anointed one and the firstborn, a servant, and a soldier.*

> *Jesus saith unto them, Did ye never read in scriptures: The stone which the builders rejected, the same is become the head of the corner. This is the Lord's doing, and it is marvelous in our eyes. Matthew 21:42-44*

Jesus Christ was the stone that the builders of His time rejected. If their relationship with God was up to date, they would not have rejected Jesus Christ. God had allowed the Jewish nation to be taken over by the Roman Empire because of their constant rebellion and gross idolatry against God's moral law. Time after time again God would deliver them from their oppressors and every time they would go back to idol worship. We live in a time when people want to re-establish God's moral boundaries, by bringing in their lifestyles and convincing themselves that God loves them too much, to punish them for breaking His moral law. God has never moved His moral boundaries or changed His laws and principles for any creature at any time.

There are no loopholes in God's moral law, we either obey and be blessed or we disobey and get punished. We constantly hear about people in court to seek exoneration for not obeying the law because they don't want the law to have jurisdiction over their behavior for operating outside of its moral composition. They don't consider or even care if God is against what they are doing, as long as they can do what they want to do. The last they want to hear from anyone is that the word of God does not condone their behavior.

On the other hand, the world doesn't have to worry about trying to cancel Christian culture, because Christians are doing that all by themselves. Through all of the immoral behavior and platforms, we have allowed the boundaries of the moral compass to be moved within the walls of Christianity through acceptance and inclusion. So now, if you don't accept certain behaviors that don't align with the word of God, you are not showing the love of God. When we begin to accept and include people into the body of Christ who embrace lifestyles and behaviors that contradict the word of God without any signs of repentance or remorse, this will be the beginning of the moral freefall of the church. This is the mentality that brought the nation of Israel under Roman rule. They didn't want God to rule over them, so God allowed the Roman Empire to become their ruler and authoritarians. They were so blind and backslidden they were unable to recognize when Jesus Christ their Messiah had finally come. They rejected every sign that God gave them concerning His Son and all the prophecies, from His birth, to His death, burial, and resurrection. He was the Eben Stone, the Bane Son, the builder of the family name.

> *For this cause I bow my knees unto the Father of our Lord Jesus Christ, of whom the whole family in heaven and earth is named.*
> *Ephesians 3:14*

The scripture firmly says that the name of the whole family in heaven and earth is Lord Jesus Christ. To become a member of this family, we must do what the spiritual leaders of Jesus's day refused to do which is to accept every sign that God has given concerning His Son and all the prophecies from His birth, to His death, burial, and resurrection.

Jesus is also the anointed one and the firstborn. He was also a servant and a soldier. They rejected Him as the head of the corner and the builder of the family name for the nation of Israel. By His death, burial and resurrection, He became the spiritual builder of the family name to the Gentiles as well as the Jews. Through Cavalry, He started a whole new family that included those who were not Jews by natural birth, but by spiritual birth.

> *That at that time ye were without Christ, being aliens from the commonwealth of Israel, and strangers from the covenants of promise, having no hope, and without God in the world. Ephesians 2:12*

This was the state of the Gentiles before Jesus came and died and brought in a better hope. Paul said the new order and under the new covenant, a Jew is no longer one outwardly by the letter, but inwardly through circumcision of the heart.

> *Now therefore ye are no more strangers and foreigners, but fellow citizens with the saints, and of the household of God; And are built upon the foundation of the apostles and prophets, Jesus Christ himself being the chief corner stone. Ephesians 2:19-20*

Jesus Christ, the Bane Son, and builder of the family name is also called the firstborn.

For whom he did foreknow, he also did predestinate to be conformed into the image of his Son, that he might be the firstborn among many brethren. Romans 8:29

This is referring to the brethren of the new covenant, the born-again brethren. In biblical Jewish history, the firstborn received the blessing of the birthright which included the king, prophet, and priestly anointing. We can see that Jesus operated in all three of these capacities. As stated in Colossians 1:18 and Revelation 1:5, He is firstborn from the dead. Being firstborn from the dead doesn't mean that He was the first to be resurrected because we saw when He raised Lazarus, when He raised Jarius' daughter, and when He raised the young son of a widow in Nain from the dead before He was crucified and only God knows how many others He raised from the dead that were not recorded. But what it means is that He was the firstborn to be resurrected by the glory of the Father and cannot die again. The people He raised from the dead during His earthly ministry all died again. When we are resurrected by the glory of the Father, we will have on resurrected bodies and death will never again have power over us because we can't die anymore. As said in Hebrews 12:23, He is also the firstborn of the church.

The stone that the builders rejected was also the anointed one. Jesus was the anointed one that was sent from the Father above to give eternal freedom to the entire human race.

The Spirit of the Lord is upon me, because he hath anointed me to preach the gospel to the poor; he hath sent me to heal the brokenhearted, to preach deliverance to the captives, and recovering of sight to the blind, to set at liberty them that are bruised, To preach the acceptable year of the Lord. Luke 4:18

But made himself of no reputation, and took on him the form of a servant and was made in the likeness of men. Philippians 2:7

The stone that the builders rejected was also a servant stone. Jesus laid aside His kingly, heavenly splendor and dawned Himself in a garment of flesh with the appearance of a common man. He came to Earth as a servant and that is why the religious leaders of His day could not recognize Him, because He didn't come in the exalted form and deliver them from the Roman yoke. The Father sent Jesus to deliver them from the inner yoke of sin, a yoke much more powerful than an outward Roman yoke. Jesus said that the, "Son of Man came not to be served, but to serve and give his life a ransom for many." Mk.10:45

How often have we missed the servant stone because He came in a way we weren't expecting and so we rejected the servant stone? He communicates with us on the level of human beings. God always comes to us in the likeness of men. We don't always accept the likeness of the person that God appears to us in because of pride and partiality that dictates to God who we will accept and who we will reject. The stone that the builders rejected was also a soldier. Jesus was the greatest soldier the earth has ever witnessed.

Greater love hath no man than this, that a man lay down his life for his friends. John 15:13

There have been many brave and valiant soldiers from every nation under heaven from generation to generation. But it has never been recorded in the history books of mankind that a soldier died for his comrades and came back to testify to them about it. This is why Jesus Christ stands out from the rest; He is the only one who has defeated death, which still holds captive all of the other great soldiers down through the ages. And the sound of His victory was not only a triumph for time but also for the eternal ages to come. Jesus not only died on Calvary but He went down into the regions of darkness and fought with all the powers of darkness and the demonic host. He took the keys of death and hell before He left and secured eternal salvation and redemption for the entire human race. Now death and hell no longer have any power over the souls of human beings because the keys have been taken from them. And in due time all souls will be released from death and hell and delivered to their final destination. This is the stone that those builders rejected and that stone has traveled down through the ages and has been rejected by the vast majority of every generation.

Now we are the builders and the Eben Stone has come to our generation and to our time to see if we will accept or reject Him. He doesn't always come in a way that we can recognize but He will always come in the form of a man. You and I must choose to either accept or reject the Eben Stone and the Bane Son, the builder of the family name. Will we allow Him to build the family name? Or will it be said of us as the builders of our generation, "This is the stone that the builders rejected?" The only sure way to make the right decision is to keep the incense of your morning and evening sacrifice ascending to God day by day. Let the fragrance of your relationship rise like smoke to the Eben Stone and the Bane Son and you will become more acquainted with how He is working in your life and then you will recognize Him when He comes in blessings and sufferings. His goal is always to build the family name inside and out. The builders of Jesus's day proved they hated the Father when they rejected and killed the stone that came in the Father's name.

CHAPTER 9

To Consider

Morning also means to consider. Consider means to think on with care, to measure the consequences, and fix the mind on a view to a careful examination. The psalmist asked God to consider His meditation.

> *Give ear to my words, O LORD, consider my meditation. My voice shalt thou hear in the morning, O LORD; in the morning will I direct my prayer unto thee, and will look up. Psalms 5:1, 3*

What are you meditating on when you awake in the morning? Wherever your meditation is, that is where your conversation will be directed. Just as the children of Israel were on a natural journey from Egypt to Canaan land, we too are on a spiritual journey from the Egypt of this world to fairer worlds on high. We must be continually reminding ourselves that we are just visitors on Earth; our stay is short and brief and we must not attach ourselves to the things of this world because we will not want to turn loose of it when it is our time to leave. We must make a careful examination of our daily activities and fellowship and in so doing, we will be able to measure the consequences.

When the children of Israel came to Mount Sinai, it was there that the Lord spoke the Ten Commandments out of thick darkness. The general assembly didn't want to hear directly from the voice of God, so they asked Moses to go for them while they stood far off. God was proving them at Sinai to see what was in their hearts and to see if they would walk by His commandments. Their actions showed God, they didn't want a close examination of the conditions of their hearts. Since they were standing so far off, the voice of the Lord had receded and they could barely hear what He was saying. They could not obey a voice they didn't want to hear. They must have thought that choosing Moses to hear God for them would make them less accountable for the law that God was speaking directly to each of them.

How often have we gone to the house of God with no real desire to be there and to hear the Word of God? We stood afar off in our desire to hear and obey the voice of God. When our desire to please God is in recession, so will be our ability to hear and obey. It wasn't long after that God told Moses to come up to the top of Mount Sinai to receive the Ten Commandments.

Not long after Moses went up to get the stones, the Israelites made graven images and gave those idols the credit for what God had done. "These be the gods which have brought us up out of Egypt." How morally depraved and mentally enslaved they had become to the sinful passions of idol worship. Had they not stood afar off when God was speaking the Torah, they would have been aware of the law that said, "Thou shalt have no other gods before me and thou shalt not make unto you any graven images." They would have taken a careful examination to measure the consequences of such actions with the understanding that they would be punished if they did.

How quickly they forgot how good God had been to them in Egypt when He put Pharaoh, the Egyptians, and the entire land of Egypt on full display through an array of plagues, one after another, while none of those plagues came near the dwellings of the children of Israel.

Consider carefully all the doors that God has opened for us, even before we gave our life to Jesus Christ. He delivered us from the death angel by allowing mercy to push back the punishment we deserved, knowing that one day we would accept Him as our Savior. We must carefully examine the Red Seas He has parted for us and the many bitter waters He made sweet. To listen to His voice for ourselves and not depend on someone else to hear what God wants to speak directly to us is the appropriate thing to do. God wanted to speak directly to each one of them and they missed it.

When Moses came down from Mount Sinai, he became angry at the sins of the people, casting down the law in stone and breaking them. Jesus descended from heaven with the law written in His heart and they crucified Him, casting Him down into death but they could not make Him break the law in His heart. And by Jesus keeping the law, He made it possible for us to do the same. Even when we are broken by testing and trials, we can still keep the law without breaking it by the grace that comes through Jesus Christ. Now that we have the law living and abiding on the inside of us through Jesus Christ, we can render better obedience to the law than those who lived in past dispensations. This is the dispensation of grace and truth that came by Jesus Christ. We must be willing to hear what God wants to say to us no matter how tough it may be. Our salvation depends on us hearing from God and obeying His voice; only then can we give ear to a careful examination of ourselves, think on it with care, and then measure the consequences of the choices we make.

CHAPTER 10

Finding Grace in His Sight

Noah was a righteous man in his generation that found grace in the sight of the Lord. One of the meanings for grace is unmerited favor. Noah found unmerited favor in the eyes of the Lord for himself and his family. It means that he did not and could not do anything to earn the unmerited favor of God. Grace gives us blessing and unmerited favor we don't deserve, while mercy pushes back the punishment we do deserve. This is the same kind of grace and mercy that has been working on our behalf throughout our lifetime. One of the meanings for the word found is sufficient. Noah found that the Lord's grace was sufficient to save his entire household.

But Noah found grace in the eyes of the LORD. Genesis 6:8

He built an ark by the commandment of the Lord and saved his family from the judgmental flood that God had promised to send upon those who inhabited the earth during that time. The word of God said that the earth was filled with violence. Many of your family and friends are still here because the grace you have found with the Lord has been sufficient enough to keep them alive. This is the reason why we have to live a devoted and committed life to Christ. I believe there is an allotted portion of souls that

God has ordained for you and me to reach and their eternal salvation may very well depend on whether or not we find grace in the sight of the Lord on their behalf.

There were eight people saved out of that entire generation, but that doesn't mean the opportunity for many more to be saved wasn't available. Noah preached for 120 years and they still refused to listen. Our responsibility is to find grace in the eyes of the Lord and be a living testimony of that same grace. Some will listen and some will not listen. But we are not responsible for those who choose not to listen because just like in Noah's day they have the same opportunity as everyone else to enter into the ark of salvation.

We are alive today because someone found grace in the sight of the Lord and prayed for us when our soul was sick and dying, bound in sin and shame. We were out doing our own thing and going our own way until one day, the grace of God that brings salvation came and rescued us, and we entered into the ark of eternal safety.

We have a responsibility before God to continue to pray for those who are on the outside of the ark of salvation. It doesn't matter who it is, how deep or wide a person's offenses, or what kind of sin they are involved in and to what degree, the power of God can deliver them just like He delivered us. His grace is sufficient to reach where they are, and bring them out from under the burden of sin. "Where sin did abound, grace did much more abound" (Rom. 5:20) they just need someone to find grace in the sight of the Lord for them. We who have already accepted Jesus Christ are witnesses of His unmerited favor and the power of His deliverance. This is why He has chosen us to be willing vessels that will find His grace for someone else. Just as we were the recipients of grace, we have to also give back our time, energy, and prayers so that others can become recipients of the same.

Our eternal destiny cannot take second place to anything, and finding grace in His sight must become a daily obsession. The door of the ark of salvation is going to close for all eternity very soon. We must visit our plans for eternity daily by finding grace in God's sight for ourselves and others.

CHAPTER 11

Good Before Evil

When God placed Adam in the garden of Eden, He gave him command of what trees to eat of and the tree he could not eat of. The Tree of Knowledge of Good and Evil was the only tree of which they could not eat. God did not say the tree of knowledge of evil and good but the tree of good and evil. There was a reason why God used that order and mentioned good before evil.

> *But of the tree of the knowledge of good and evil, thou shalt not eat of it: for in the day that thou eatest thereof thou shalt surely die. Genesis 2:17*

> *Then the eyes of both of them were opened, and they knew that they were naked; and sewed fig leaves together to make themselves aprons. Genesis 3:7*

These are eyes that were opened out of season by an act of rebellion. Because they stole from the tree they were commanded not to eat of, and now what God says is good we call evil and what God calls evil we call good. When they took from the tree of knowledge out of season, the order was reversed and directly opposite to God's original intentions of seeing good before evil. When they ate of the forbidden tree, they saw evil before they could see good. We are admonished to not be overcome with evil, but overcome evil with good. When we are eating from the wrong tree, all we can see is what we don't like about someone or something.

We all have experienced certain people we have struggled trying to love and have displayed very negative attitudes toward them, and have not treated them the same as we have others. Until we get serious about dealing with our wrong order of evil before good, nothing will change. We cannot continue to use excuses of why we treat them the way we do, because if we argue for our excuses we get to keep them, and if we keep our excuses, we will also keep our negative behavior toward others. The Christ in us has eyes to see the good in things. When we are as concerned about how we are treating some, as we are about how we treat everyone else, only then can the order be reversed back to the way God intended for it to be, good and evil.

Be not overcome with evil, but overcome evil with good. Romans 12:21

As we begin to spend more time in God's presence and the Word of God, we will find it easier to look for the good in others because that's what Jesus, the living Word, does to all of His creation. Through the living Word, we will be able to see people the same way God sees them. The more we grow, the more good we will see, and the more good we see about a person the more we will be able to use that to overcome the evil or the bad and negative things about them.

Butter and honey shall he eat, that he may know to refuse the evil, and choose the good. Isaiah 7:15

Butter and honey is a picture of the Word of God that we have to eat so that we may learn how to refuse to look at the evil in people and choose to see the good in them. The living Word became flesh in an infant form before He grew to adulthood. That is why the apostle Peter said,

> *As newborn babes desire the sincere milk of the word that ye may grow thereby. 1 Peter 2:2*

We are commanded to grow so that one day we may become spiritual adults. It is a childish thing to constantly have evil thoughts toward someone just because we don't want to assume the responsibility of growing up and becoming a mature Christian, to where we can think and do good toward them.

> *When I was a child, I spoke as a child, I understood as a child, I thought as a child: but when I became a man, I put away childish things. 1 Corinthians 13:11*

After the fall of our fore-parents, we inherited a fallen nature that always sees evil before good. Jesus Christ, the living Word, will transform us by imparting to us His divine nature that will allow us to act just like Him and to have His Father's eyes to always see the good in all of His creation.

> *And God saw everything that he had made, and, behold, it was very good. And the evening and the morning was the sixth day. Genesis 1:31*

After each day of creation, God looked at what He had created and said that it was good. But on the sixth day, He looked at everything and said it was very good. As we continue on our journey with God and continue to allow Him to transform us through His Word, we will eventually come to a place in our walk with Christ where we can look and see creation the way God sees it. Then we will be able to say what God says. It's good in its singleness, but very good in its collectivity.

CHAPTER 12

To Care For

Morning also *means to care for*. When you care for someone, you do all you can to nourish that relationship and supply whatever is lacking for the present and future success of the relationship. When we refuse to take the time to offer our morning sacrifices to God, we are making a visible, nonverbal demonstration to the Lord of just how much we care for the present and future success of our relationship with Him. Yes, we do have acceptable excuses sometimes, but to use a myriad of excuses just to excuse oneself from the presence of the Lord is unacceptable. You need to prove to God how much you care about being in a relationship with Him. The proof of how much we care is in our choices more so than our voices. God sees your choice at face value, not what you say.

What kind of sacrifice are you willing to make for Jesus? He made the ultimate sacrifice for you. Are you willing to begin today to set aside some time and prove to Him how much you care about being in a relationship with Him? Will you let your incense rise unto Him, morning and evening? Maybe initially, you don't think you can be faithful morning and evening. Start being faithful to just one, morning or evening, and when you establish faithfulness in the morning, ask God to make you faithful to your evening sacrifice as well. He will work with you, just like He did for me. Even if you start out spending only five minutes a day; if you are faithful, that's a strong start.

It all depends on how much you are willing to give up to go on that kind of journey. Are you willing to lose your relationship with some of your friends and family if Jesus calls you to make that kind of sacrifice, to gain a much greater relationship with Him? Just to be clear as to the point I am making, I'm not talking about turning your back on friends and family, but to be more separated unto God will require you to spend more time with Him, which will result in spending less time with them; even if you don't have the will or desire to do it but you know that you need to. You can pray like this, "Lord, I am willing to be made willing." That is how I was taught to pray. And if you do it with sincerity, God will use such a feeble prayer and carry you until the desire comes.

There are times in the life of a sincere Christian that God may remove them out of familiar settings so that He can work within them, a greater desire and commitment to service. God separates us from different people, for different reasons, and at different times so that we don't miss our seasons to grow in our relationship with God. As we begin to care for our relationship with Christ in a greater way, we must also care for the brotherhood. Jesus said that all men will know that we are His disciples if we have loved one another. We can't properly and appropriately care for our relationship with Christ without having that same kind of care for the brotherhood.

> *So we, being many, are one body in Christ, and every one members of one of another. Romans 12:5*

God has so ordained that we care for one another as if we are caring for our very own body and do nothing that will cause a self-inflicted injury or ill will to the body. We are to show care in our giving to the needs of others, as the Lord leads us to do so. Where we lack in substance we can make up for in prayer, and perhaps God will hear the substance of our prayer and will put it on someone to give of their substance in equal proportion to the prayer that was offered. Sometimes, He gives abundantly over and above all we have asked or ever could have imagined.

We also care for our relationship with Christ Jesus by repenting of sinful deeds and habits. When we sincerely care for our relationship with the Lord Jesus Christ, we will allow nothing or no one between our soul and our Savior. Sin breaks our communion with God. I am talking about willful, sinful behavior. Presumptuous sins are when one has full knowledge of God's Word and the consequences that go along with it, concerning what not to do, and does it anyway. For if we sin willfully, there no longer remains a sacrifice for sin. Paul had to reprove the saints at Corinth for willful, sinful behavior in the church.

> *Your glorying is not good. Know ye not that a little leaven leaveneth the whole lump? Purge out therefore the old leaven that ye may be a new lump, as ye are unleavened. For even Christ our Passover is sacrificed for us: Therefore let us keep the feast, not with old leaven, neither with the leaven of malice and wickedness; but with the unleavened bread of sincerity and truth. 1 Corinthians 5:6-8*

The leaven of the sin of fornication had crept into the church in a big way at Corinth and Paul began to admonish them to purge out this old leaven (or sinful practice) and be a new lump. Paul compared the leavened bread to malice and wickedness and he compared the unleavened bread to sincerity and truth. Unleavened Bread was eaten with the Passover on the fourteenth day of the first month and celebrated at the same time as part of a joint commemoration, part of the same picture, and the same overall experience. You cannot have one without the other. Although unleavened bread was eaten with the Passover, the feast of unleavened bread did not begin until the fifteenth day of the same month. Moses was commanded to observe the Feast of Unleavened Bread the day after the Passover. For seven days they were to observe the Feast of Unleavened Bread and no leaven was to be found in their houses during that time.

When leaven is applied to dough, it causes the bread to rise and it only takes a little bit of leaven to make a whole lump of dough rise. That is exactly how sin works both in the individual and in the body of Christ. It only takes a little bit of sin going unchecked and unreproved, then it won't be long before the whole body is affected by that type of behavior. This is why leaven is likened to malice and wickedness because it represents sinful deeds and actions working in the body of Christ and the perpetrators by indulging in just a little leaven of sinful practice. The whole body will suffer naturally and spiritually as a result.

The only way to truly keep the feast is by purging out the sinful leaven of malice and wickedness. When God says not to touch or gives a command not to do a certain thing, He means exactly what He says. No one, regardless of rank, authority, or position of power, has been given special permission from God to disobey His Word. Repentance is how we keep the feast and how we purge out the old leaven and become a new lump. When we partake of the bread of sincerity and truth, we will become sincere and truthful. The unleavened bread of sincerity and truth is the only bread that God has given us to eat the Passover with. "For even Christ our Passover is sacrificed for us, therefore let us keep the feast. (1 Cor. 5:7-8) By partaking in the Passover Lamb with the bread of sincerity and truth, we show God just how much we care for our relationship with Him.

CHAPTER 13

To Inquire

Morning also means to inquire, which means to *meditate.* Meditation is the key that unlocks the door of worship into God's presence for a time of divine fellowship. The psalmist said, "My meditation of him shall be sweet." It is impolite to just come into the presence of the Lord and cast all of our problems and concerns at His feet without first taking some time to thank and praise Him for things the way they are. Always give homage to the king before you ask any request of Him.

> *Be anxious for nothing, but in everything, by prayer and supplication with thanksgiving, let your requests be made known unto God. Philippians 4:6*

Paul said that our prayers, supplications, and thanksgiving should come first before we make our request to Him. By doing this, we establish a respectful approach to His presence and the proper way to cast our cares on Him. We must come before Him with a profound sense of reverence and gratitude for just the privilege of being in a relationship with Him. I do, however, believe that there are times when our soul may be so overwhelmed with the burdens of life that our need for God to move is so urgent and pressing that we immediately begin to beg God for help we need in that moment. Meditation also means to be in close association, to be agreeable, and to be pleasant. The psalmist had pleasant memories of his close association with God and he was agreeable with how God was running the affairs of his life. Our meditation isn't really sweet until we can be agreeable with how God is controlling our life.

> *More to be desired are they than gold, yea, than much fine gold: sweeter also than honey and the honeycomb. Psalm 19:10*

The extent to which we desire to have fellowship with God will be in direct proportion to the amount of time we are willing to set aside to make it happen. The sweeter the meditation the more time we will spend in His presence. There we will learn how to be agreeable with God, even when the circumstances of life don't look like what we are agreeing with. We are agreeing with God's choice to use circumstances to bring us into closer proximity with Him. To bring us back into fellowship with Himself, God has to reform and restore us.

The reforming and restoring process is a journey of character makeover. In His presence is where we are reformed and made new and restored into fellowship with God. There can be no proper restoration in our life until there is first a reformation. *Reformation means rebirth, to be reborn and corrected in a pattern of behavior.* God cannot properly restore the human race to a relationship with Him until He first reforms us through a born-again experience that will correct our pattern of behavior.

Reformation is usually connected with inward change of flaws and character deficiency. Through appointed circumstances, He reforms us by working in us and removing character flaws, spots, and blemishes that are not Christ-like, and replacing our deficiencies with Christ-like qualities that was lacking before the reformation process began. He changes our way of thinking so that in the days ahead we can make better decisions when faced with similar circumstances.

This is why we sometimes fall into the same sinful activity over and over again. What we seek first is restoration before the reformation. We want to be restored to a position before we have been reformed of the inward deficiency and unchristlike character that made us fall in the first place. What good is it for anyone to be restored to the position without change? Without the removal of inward flaws, spots, and blemishes and correction in behavior, everything remains the same. We will continue without showing any effects or signs of change that will prevent previous activity from reoccurring.

It is sometimes hard to accept tough criticism of ourselves because it may suggest giving up something we don't want to let go of; so we will only be honest about ourselves to a certain degree. Too much of our pride is on the line and the sacrifice we need to make will not allow us to cooperate with the kind of criticism we need to hear, to start the reforming process. The truest form of restoration cannot be achieved until the process of reformation is completed. But when we learn the secret of sweet meditation, our only desire is to be in close association with Him and have an agreeable and pleasant relationship with the Savior, regardless of the degree of criticism I need to hear if that's what it takes to have that kind of fellowship with the Lord.

Positions of ministry and leadership will take a back seat in the reforming process until being in fellowship with Jesus Christ is more to be desired than much fine gold of ministry and is sweeter than the honeycombs of positions. That's when the reforming process is at its best and that is not to belittle positions of ministry, it's just that your relationship with Jesus supersedes ministry. Ministry will flow freely out of a relationship that has been through the reforming process and properly restored.

There is an appointed time for reformation.

> *Which stood only in meats and drinks, and divers washings, and carnal ordinances, imposed on them until the time of reformation. Hebrews 9:10*

Under the old covenant, the individual could not experience the full effect of inward change because the law could not make him perfect pertaining to the conscience. This is just another way of saying it could not reform them from within. They had to render obedience to the law from without and that without the help of grace and truth. Grace and truth transform us from within and helps govern the outflow of our conduct. "The law was given by Moses but grace and truth came by Jesus Christ" (John 1:17). Grace and truth came to assist God in writing the law in our hearts which is the full purpose for the time of reformation.

Jesus Christ was and is the only one who practiced perfect obedience to the moral law of thou shalt and thou shalt not. And now that He has performed this kind of obedience in His body, He can come into our hearts as an incorruptible seed of righteousness, with all of the Godly attributes and abilities to grow inside of us until He produces the same kind of obedience within us. He allows grace and truth to give us a margin for error. Therefore, because of grace and truth, we are convicted and convinced of sin instead of condemned by the law; we are not under the law but grace.

The time of reformation is about having the same moral law written in our hearts by grace and truth instead of on tables of stone. God removes the heart of stone which was written under the old covenant and He gives us a heart of flesh to write the same law but under a better covenant. So we should not get discouraged because we sometimes fail in keeping the law. Grace and truth will continue to pick us up when we fall and speak words of life to us and will not stop working with us until they work in and through us the obedience the law demands. As we assume the responsibility of offering up our incense both morning and evening, we will find the transcending, transforming power to meet every single challenge of the dawning of this new era of darkness and uncertainty. We must live every day with a desire and expectancy of hearing the Savior say, "Well done, thy good and faithful servant."

CHAPTER 14

To Admire

The word for *morning means to admire and to be lovely*. The tabernacle is where God's presence dwelt.

How amiable are thy tabernacle. Psalm 84:1

So what the psalmist was saying is, "How lovely is your dwelling place."

LORD, I have loved the habitation of thy house, and the place where thine honor dwelleth. Psalm 26:8

The more we choose to give ourselves to offering our incense the more lovely our relationship and experience with God will be, and the more we will admire His dwelling place.

The Mosaic Tabernacle in the wilderness was a temporary dwelling place for the presence of the Lord. It was sufficient for the time then present until King Solomon built the temple in Jerusalem, a permanent place for the name of the Lord to rest and abide. God wants to have a permanent dwelling place within you and me, so He can make our temple a place where His honor dwells. Our body is the temple of God and it doesn't matter how messed up your life may be, it doesn't matter how many wrong choices you have made, how many times you have fallen, or how ugly your situation looks, He can make your temple a lovely dwelling place for His presence to abide and a place where His honor dwells. We are not complete in our relationship with Christ until our temple becomes a place where His honor dwells. God wants us to walk in such a way that others will admire His presence within us. I believe these six Godly characteristics will help us get there.

> *Finally brethren, whatsoever things are true, whatsoever things are honest, whatsoever things are just, whatsoever things are pure, whatsoever things are lovely, whatsoever things are of good report; if there be any virtue, and if there be any praise, think on these things. Philippians 4:8*

These are the noble qualities that He will work within us so that our temple can become a place for His honor to dwell.

Truth–There are no shadows of turning with the truth. There is no such thing as my truth and your truth; there is only one truth. God established truth before He created anything. Truth is a person, the Son of God, the Lord Jesus Christ. Jesus said, "I am the way, the truth and the life." We will one day stand in God's court and be judged by His truth. If our final judgment is His truth, then that is what our behavior should be governed by now. Our actions should be aligned with what we want our final judgement to be.

If we want our so called version of the truth to rule now, it will not stand in God's court; we will be condemned when we stand before God's truth in the final judgment. But if we take God's truth now, it will justify us in the final judgement. When we have a relationship with the truth, we honor the Father through that relationship. Love for the truth will say that

God is still good even when situations don't agree with what we are saying. If we are going to make truth our companion then we must learn how to defend truth regardless of how bad the situation looks because situations come and go, but truth endures forever. Truth has its very origin in the heavenly Father. Jesus Christ was the express image of the invisible God, which means that everything He said and did was an expression of what the invisible Father was saying and doing.

> *Who being the brightness of his glory, and the express image of his person, and upholding all things by the word of his power, when he had by himself purged our sins, sat down on the right hand of the Majesty on high. Hebrews 1:3*

And He came and subjected Himself to the conditions of the time for a season, but now He is at the right hand of the Majesty on high. And just because some may not choose to believe in the truth now, doesn't mean they have gotten away with anything. God isn't going to stop being God just because some of His subjects don't want to accept His position of authority over their existence. God has given every human being an allotment of time to choose the truth and if they don't, when it is their time to say goodbye to planet Earth, God will make the choices for them and His truth will keep marching on.

Truth is not what we know about a subject but what God knows about that subject. We may know about a wrong someone has done and that is true from our point of view, especially if it touches us. If they sincerely repent and do business with God, then He forgives them. It doesn't mean that they have gotten away with wrong just because God didn't punish them the way we wanted to see them punished, it just means that God has accepted their repentance. He is still a just judge and He will measure out a just judgment for their action.

He will not, however, allow them to be accused before Him again for the same offense. Sometimes, His mercy overrides the offense and He doesn't punish them at all just as He has done for us on many occasions. The reason we don't want God to show the same kind of mercy to others that He showed us is that it hurts our pride and invalidates our assessment of them in the eyes of others. When we choose to allow truth to be all that it should be, it eliminates the question of John the Baptist, "Are you the one, or look we for another?" (Matt. 11:3).

Honest–*To be honest means that you are sincere and do not knowingly practice deceit, lies, hypocrisy, and untruthfulness; and it also means the absence of lying, cheating, and stealing.* Honesty is a desirable characteristic that God will work in us to bring His presence near. It is a condition of moral character that will not allow you to be any other way. It always sees itself as a winner regardless of what loss may be incurred in the process. To a person of integrity, winning and losing are from God's point of view, period. A person of honesty will not even consider getting away with something just because no one else can see or know about it; they are always Christ-conscious and aware that the eyes of the Lord are always open to all things in all places and at all times. Those who embrace the moral character of honesty don't live a double standard. They are who they are when no one else is watching; whoever they are in your presence, that is who they are in your absence. This is the honest and desirable quality of character to pray for and long for.

Just–To be just is to behave based on what is morally right and fair and to judge with an unbiased weight. A just person is lawful and upright. Someone who is just is clear of the offense of the law. To be morally right is to be legally right from God's point of view. What is moral is also legal from

God's point of view. The legality of the law was supposed to be adopted from a moral compass. Even Martin Luther King said, "When man's law becomes aligned with God's law, only then can the world become a just place to live in." And I know we live in a nation where legalizing immorality is getting to be the new normal. But according to the scriptures, it has to be that way because it is the fulfillment of prophecy that Jesus spoke, "As it were, so shall it be."

The God of Israel said, the Rock of Israel spoke to me, He that ruleth over men must be just, ruling in the fear of God. 2 Samuel 23:3

These were the words of David after God made him king in Israel. In so many words, God told the new king that a just man must live by the same standard of laws he judges others by. Could this be the reason why there is such a problem in church leadership, in business, and in the home?

Too often we don't live by the same standards that we judge by. We must be inwardly reformed to what is morally right so that we can set by example standards of justice as boundaries of how we deal with people. A just man is not partial in judgment and he doesn't consider those who have more above those who have less, nor does he take sides with those who give more over those who give less. The just man understands the meaning of equity from personal conviction not by outward influence.

...and to the spirits of just men made perfect. Hebrews 12:23

To be perfect means that it is finished and that it lacks nothing necessary for completeness. Although our spirits will not experience the fullness of perfection until we get to heaven, yet, we can experience it in a measure. The spirits of just men are equitable in character, righteous in judgment, holy in disposition, and are clear of all wrong in the eyes of God. Right here is another stand you have to make for your spiritual freedom. When God cleanses your spirit from sin and guilt, the devil will come back to try you to see if you are going to live in the fullness of that freedom or if he can snatch it away from you by recalling your faults.

Remember his very nature is to accuse and all he has with him is an accusing voice with no truth, no honesty, and no justice attached to it because he doesn't want your spirit to be made perfect. And you can't be silent, you have to get loud with the devil because if you don't, he will roar at you with his accusations until he overcome you and you put back on a robe of guilt that God has already taken from you. The just shall live by faith and the spirit of just men are free of any condemnation. "There is therefore now no condemnation to them which are in Christ Jesus, who walk not after the flesh, but after the Spirit" (Rom. 8:1). You are the one to determine when you want to be free of condemnation. I will give you a hint, the key word in that scripture is *now*. And if now is your choice, you must forcefully convey that to your adversary, the devil, and resist him with a strong verbal declaration and he will flee from you.

Pure–*Is to be unmixed or unadulterated with any other substance; to be free of contamination; a person without malice, treachery, or evil intent, sincere and without guile.* A Christian who seeks and desires a pure character does not seek fellowship with the world.

> *...know ye not that friendship with the world is enmity toward God? James 4:4*

Contrary to how some people think, this scripture isn't saying that we can't have worldly friends. Even Jesus said to make yourselves friends of the mammon of unrighteousness. God wants us to be friendly to everyone, but being friendly doesn't mean we hang out with them. What it means is that we are not to allow ourselves to become influenced by their worldly lifestyle. Because it leaves the wrong impression of what a Christian is supposed to be and how they are supposed to live. It is an embarrassment to the name of Jesus when the world has to reprove us of how we should be living.

If there is a double standard in the world toward Christians that's only because the double standard existed in the church first, and now we are reaping what has been sown. We are not saying that it is wrong to be with family and friends for times of good and wholesome fun, but you should be careful that you don't allow your actions to misrepresent your Christian values. If their ways are of the world we should not desire to do the things they do or go the places they go just to fit in momentarily, so that our good is not evil spoken of by those who are watching and know how we are supposed to conduct ourselves. It is important not to taint our relationship with the Savior through worldly friendships. Do not make deals with them like if you go to the club or party with them, they will go to church with you. We can't go to the devil's playground without eventually playing with some of his toys. Those who are pure do not mix with those who are impure by choice.

> *Wherefore come out from among them, and be ye separate saith the Lord, and touch not the unclean thing, and I will receive you.*
> *2 Corinthians 6:17*

God wants to give us such a pure nature that it carries over in every aspect of our lives and our actions. He wants pureness to be in the details of our lives so that we deal with the very thought of impure things. The main reason why we fall into certain types of sins is that we leave God out of the details and our thoughts are not pure. We don't commit any sin until we first have thought about it (that's the detail of our actions). After the impure thoughts we enjoy the impure feelings and then we crave some impure action. As God works the pureness of His nature within us by helping us obey His word and memorize scripture, we will learn to channel our energy to think on pure things, and then we will have pure feelings and actions. Those who desire to be pure will learn a pure language that will flow from a pure heart. Gratitude is the only language that doesn't have flaws because it's a pure language and God's ears are always open to a pure language.

> *For then will I turn to the people a pure language, that they may all call upon the name of the LORD, to serve him with one consent. Ephesians 3:9*

> *And in their mouth was found no guile: for they are without fault before the throne of God. Revelation 14:5*

To be pure is to be without guile. If we desire to be presented without fault before the throne of God we must not practice guile, which is trickery, a sly and cunning way of dealing with people. It is the pure character and nature of Jesus Christ within us that will be presented faultless and without blame before the throne of God. The only way Jesus can present us blameless before the Father is that we have to learn how to present Him blameless in the situations and circumstances of life, by giving Him thanks for everything He allows us to go through without murmuring and complaining and accusing Him of being unfair about how He is directing our path. If we sow presenting Him blameless in time, we will reap Him presenting us blameless throughout eternity.

Lovely–*Is pleasing, agreeable, acceptable, and grateful.* This speaks directly to the inner nature and character of the Lord Jesus Christ and gives us a glimpse of His very person. Having a spiritual beauty and a grateful disposition that gives grace to those who are present is what it means to be lovely. A person who has this quality on display in their lives forgives when done wrong and is willing to start afresh and anew with the one who offended. (Although it may not happen right away, eventually it will). To be lovely means that you don't resist being around someone who has offended you in the past. This is how God showed forth His lovely nature to the offender under the old testament order. The high priest in the old testament tabernacle wore a miter with blue lace and inside the lace was the writing of a signet, *HOLINESS UNTO THE LORD*, for the holy gifts that they would bring to be offered unto the Lord out of gratitude unto Him. It let us know that even a gratitude offering was subjected to a process of sanctification before God would accept it. That is why Aaron wore *HOLINESS UNTO THE LORD* on his forehead on the front of the miter so that their offerings would always be accepted before the Lord.

> *And it shall be upon Aaron's forehead, that Aaron may bear the inquiry of the holy things, which the children of Israel shall hallow in all their holy gifts; and it shall be always upon his forehead, that they may be accepted before the LORD. Exodus 28:38*

The priest was required to live a holy life before he could wear the miter of *HOLINESS UNTO THE LORD* on his forehead. He was to be a representative of the merciful name of the Lord to the nation of Israel so that all of their gifts and sacrifices would be accepted before the Lord; especially, when it was an offering of repentance seeking forgiveness of sin out of sincerity. Therefore, God wants us to adorn ourselves with priestly garments and put on the miter of *HOLINESS UNTO THE LORD*, so that even our offenders will be accepted back into our circle of fellowship, with a temperament of humility from a lovely disposition. This is the purest reflection of Jesus Christ.

Good Report–*means excellent news.* And we are to approve excellent things.

> *And that ye may approve things that are excellent; that ye may be sincere and without offense until the day of Christ. Philippians 1:10*

When we approve excellent things we are merely approving the character and personality of the report. A good report is free of any evil intentions or interpretation. A good report consists of facts and evidence that are both relevant and necessary to support any recommendation by which the conclusion may be drawn. Caleb and Joshua were the only spies out of twelve to bring back a good report. They all came back with evidence that supported the conclusion that indeed Canaan land was good. They brought back figs, pomegranates, and a cluster of grapes that was so big that it had to be carried by two men.

> *But the men that went up with him said, we are not able to go up against the people; for they are stronger than we. And they brought up an evil report of the land they had searched unto the children of Israel, saying, "The land, through which we have gone to search it, is a land that eateth up the inhabitants thereof; and all the people we saw in it are men of great stature. Numbers 13:31-32*

All of our battles are won or lost by the medium we choose to fight them with. The ten spies were right about the giants in the land, that isn't what made their report evil. What made the report evil is when they said they are too strong for us and we cannot defeat them. After all God had done, after all the miracles He had done for them along the way, they chose to give a report contrary to Caleb and Joshua. They had a chance to approve something excellent. Their continual doubting, murmuring, and complaining did not allow them to bring back a good report and as a direct result of it, that was the straw that broke the camel's back. God gave them the due process of their constant rebellion and did not let that generation go into Canaan land.

When God has promised us something from His Word, we are to believe that He can do it for us, in us, through us; it doesn't matter how big the giants of our flesh and the giants of doubt may be. We must bring to Him a good report of faith in His Word and prove how excellent His name is in all the earth. There are promises in God's Word He has given us that we can only activate through faith, by speaking and joining our breath of faith to the promise. Release your breath of faith and watch how He will begin to move and approve some things that are excellent on your behalf.

He staggered not at the promise of God through unbelief; but was strong in faith, giving glory to God; And being fully persuaded that, what he had promised, he was able to perform. Romans 4:20-21

They entered not, because of unbelief. Hebrews 3:19

The Israelites had to wander in the wilderness until they had all died off, except four (Joshua, Phineas, Eleazer, and Caleb). Two came back with a good report. Joshua and Caleb believed that God would give them the land and fight for them and that's why they were able to bring back a good report. They had something that the other ten did not have called faith.

For by it the elders obtained a good report. Hebrews 11:2

Giving evil reports of the promises of God to the saints of God can cause others to wander in the wilderness of this world and miss out on their breakthrough season of promised blessing He has appointed for them through the evidence of faith. Having a good report is believing that God can and will do exactly what He said, in His time. Once we learn the secret of how admirable His dwelling places are, we will have faith to believe in Him to keep working with us until our temple becomes a lovely dwelling place for His presence to reside and a place where His honor dwells.

CHAPTER 15

To Seek

Morning also means to seek. Until we become transparent with ourselves we can never be that way with anyone else. The reality of our desire to seek God will be determined by how far we are willing to go in our quest to find Him, and by what measures we are willing to take to obtain the outcome to transition into that kind of relationship. We must let God choose the sacrifice of people, places, and things He wants as an offering from us. We cannot have a draw nigh experience as long we are controlling the narrative of what to put on the altar. Being in a relationship with Him means that He has the right to take us out of relationships with people, places, and things (either permanently or temporarily) until we have established the kind of relationship with Him that He desires to have with us.

One day while at work, I heard the Lord speak to me and He said, "Until you find a cause worth dying for, you will never know the true purpose of what you're living for. And when you find a cause worth dying for, then you would have found the reason for both living and dying."

You will find me when you have searched for me with all your heart.
Jeremiah 29:13

When we resolve to seek God with all of our heart, it is necessary to leave anything that will be an abstraction to our quest and detour our focus. In times when God seems so far away, in some unreachable distance, we cannot hear Him or feel the nearness of His presence. If the reason isn't because of some secret sins we are involved in then take courage. These are sacred, solitary times where God is allowing us to make cold, hard choices without any feelings attached. These are seasons in our lives where we walk alone, not without the Spirit but without the Spirit influencing us to do and to be. Why? He wants to know if we will seek Him just as fervently as we did when we were feeling His presence. He wants to know if we will be just as faithful to do the right thing without influence; He wants to know if we will continue to go to the right places and fellowship with the right circle of people without the influence.

If the reason God seems so far away is because of secret sins, we cannot just confess we have sinned, we must be specific to the sin and we have to honestly seek God to change us. The saying, confession without change is just a game, holds much weight and there is simply no time left for playing games with our eternal soul. In his book, *My Utmost for His Highest,* Oswald Chambers says the profession of sins is like falling leaves from a tree when the heart is not remorseful and sincere; "Lots of leaves, Yes, much profession, but O' how little real confession."

God is merciful and full of compassion and He gives us a chance to deal with our secret sins in the private sector of our lives. But if we refuse to repent in private where only we and God know about it, then God will expose us and allow our private life of sin into the public view and let everyone see what we were doing in secret. This will be our punishment for not repenting and doing serious business with God when we had the opportunity to do so. Jesus said,

...and your Father which seeth in secret will reward you openly. Matthew 6:4

God shall bring every work into judgment, with every secret thing, whether it be good or whether it be evil. Ecclesiastes 12:14

That goes both ways, for right and wrong. God rewards us openly with blessing when He sees our faithful obedience to His Word in secret, and He will reward us openly with judgment and shame when He sees our unfaithful disobedience in secret. Our lives should be with such transparency that if God turned the tables and made our private life public, it would reflect the same image, there would be no dark shadows to call into question. But when He has to punish us for not repenting of secret sins, He punishes us with shame and embarrassment because we didn't take advantage of the time and space He gave us to get it together. But if it takes shame and embarrassment to get our attention and rescue us from sin, we should thank and praise God for the shame of being exposed. We should thank Him for the embarrassment we felt for exposing our hypocritical lifestyle. Thank and praise Him for His mighty acts that helped us seek Him through exposure and find Him to be merciful and gracious to forgive our secret sins. The shame and embarrassment are temporary and God gives us a chance to heal and repair the breach if we are sincere. But the shame that will be felt by those who miss the rapture cannot be recovered, except they are willing to die for not taking the mark of the beast, his name, or his number.

Living in sin makes us naked before God and it is better to have the shame of our nakedness exposed now and be clothed with the garments of repentance than to have the shame of our nakedness appear at the time of the rapture and be left behind.

If so being clothed upon we shall not be found naked. 2 Corinthians 5:2

When Joseph was summoned to appear before Pharaoh, the king of Egypt, the custom was that he had to be washed and properly dressed. True and sincere repentance will allow us to be washed and properly dressed when we appear before Jesus, the King of heaven and Earth. So He rescues us through exposure to teach us how to be more transparent in our secret life. He also makes us feel shame by exposure in time so that He can honor us throughout eternity.

God also allows shame of exposure to break us so we may weep tears of sorrow and regret for the wrong we have done. The brokenness that we feel when God has to chastise us for willfully sinning against Him and not repenting is a necessary experience because it teaches us that God takes measures to discipline us seriously. He employs the rod of correction to be both our mediator and negotiator until we learn how to live in compliance with His Word and His rules. When we express sorrow and regret our sinful behavior, it isn't just because we have been exposed, but we weep because we begin to feel our offense against God's Spirit and Word. God allows our heart and soul to feel our sin the way He felt it when we sinned. And when we do we will weep the same kind of tears He wept, which is called godly sorrow. These are the tears He puts into a bottle, because when our heart and soul feel our sins the way He felt them, then our tears will match His tears. These are tears of godly sorrow.

For godly sorrow worketh repentance to salvation not to be repentant of: but the sorrow of this world worketh death. 2 Corinthians 7:10

He doesn't save tears of self-pity in a bottle. This is why He wants to hear a cry from us that will produce tears He can put in a bottle. We haven't proven to God how sorry we are for our wrongs until there are tears of godly sorrow in a bottle. Even Jesus, Himself, offered up strong crying although it was not for Him but for you and me.

> *Who in the days of his flesh, when he had offered up prayers and supplications with strong crying and tears unto him that was able to save him from death, and was heard in that he feared. Hebrews 5:7*

Jesus has left us an example to follow on how to truly seek God and be heard by Him. We need to follow Jesus's example and start offering up strong crying unto Him that can deliver us from death. God is looking for people who will sincerely seek after Him with no hidden agenda. How far are you willing to go to have a true and meaningful personal relationship with Him? What things, what people, and places are you willing to sacrifice to obtain that kind of relationship? Sometimes God doesn't want to take anything from us at all, He just wants to see if we are willing to give it up and put it on the altar, just as He did with Abraham and Isaac.

CHAPTER 16

This Poor Man Cried

We often associate the word poor with an outward condition or status quo of some unfortunate individual. But once we survey the broader meaning of the word poor, we will see ourselves and where we fit in the conversation and the status quo. *To be poor means to be unfortunate; it means to be miserable, wretched, unhappy, limited, inferior, lowly, oppressed, and crushed.* Many who are rich with outward substances are very poor when it comes to inward substances. Their outward substance does not allow them to see the inner need. They are very poor in the things that matter the most. This is similar to the mentality of big brother in the parable of the parodical son. He wasn't really big in the things that mattered most, like mercy, love, compassion and forgiveness. There's no record that he ever went in to celebrate the return of his younger brother. We will never cry for change until we can see how poor we are when it comes to practicing what we know.

> *This poor man cried, and the LORD heard him, and saved him out of all his troubles. Psalm 34:6*

We all have been guilty at one time or another of looking at the beggar on the street or the one holding a sign, "Will work for food," and shaking our heads or thinking to ourselves, "If they really will work for food, why don't they go and get a real job?" Some are holding a sign because of nothing but pure laziness, while others had unfortunate circumstances that put them there. The connection I want to make is how often do we recognize how poor we are in acting like Jesus toward others. How much time do we spend crying out to God to help us with our inner poverty? Or do we still believe that when we became Christians that we have been a true reflection of Jesus Christ since that time? We use the scripture, "If any man be in Christ he is a new creature." 1 Cor.5:17 And that is true, but there is a vast difference between Christ being in you and you being in Christ. Your initial salvation begins with Christ in you, but it is a growing process that requires dying out to the flesh before you are in Christ. So we miss opportunities to be His reflection because when it's time for Him to shine through us, we don't always allow Him to.

We consider it a weakness to show kindness to someone who doesn't like us. Whatever reason we use to justify ourselves is just an excuse for how poor we are in allowing the kind nature of Jesus Christ to shine through us. When we are arguing with someone about right and wrong, the real reason we argue is not that we want to be right; the real reason is that we are too poor in Christ's humility. We don't just disrespect people because we don't think they deserve our respect; we do it because we are too poor in allowing Christ's honor and respect to shine through us. We don't always dislike other races and cultures because of our upbringing. We dislike them simply because we are too poor in Christ's nature and character that loves all races; therefore leaving us incapable of allowing Him to manifest His love through us. When God allows us to be transacted through situations and circumstances, many times we show non-sufficient funds in our spiritual account of the nature and character of Jesus Christ that isn't enough to cover the situation.

When the rich man would not give Lazarus the crumbs that fell from his table, it wasn't only because of his pride and disregard for human life. The real reason was that he was very poor in things of eternal value that mattered the most. Although he had a wealthy account in temporal things, he had a negative balance in the eternal wealth of godly character and humility. His negative balance of brotherly kindness would not allow him to share crumbs of compassion with the poor man, Lazarus.

> *There was a certain rich man, who was clothed in purple and fine linen, and fared sumptuously every day: And there was a certain beggar named Lazarus, which was laid at his gate, full of sores, And desiring to be fed with the crumbs that fell from the rich man's table: moreover the dogs came and licked his sores. Luke 16:19-31*

When we are willing to see our inward poverty and be honest enough to own up to what God is showing us about ourselves, we will be just like the poor man who cried. How many beggars has God brought to us desiring the crumbs of mercy, the crumbs of forgiveness, crumbs of love and compassion, the crumbs of understanding and fellowship, but instead we let the dogs of our fleshly attitudes and dispositions lick the open sores of their faults and failures with criticism, and scorning, belittling and speaking negatively about them?

When we are willing to identify the areas in our life where we are not a true reflection of Jesus Christ and see how poor we are in that area of our relationship with Him, once we become desperate enough for change and realize that only God can bring that change to us, then we will cry out from our inner poverty. God wants us to be rich in kindness, rich in mercy, and rich in love, hope and peace. He wants us to be rich in the things that reflect who He is toward others.

> *For God, who is rich in mercy, for his great love wherewith he loved us, Even when we were dead in sins, hath quicken us together with Christ, (by grace are ye saved). Ephesians 2:4-5*

If we are faithful and honest to identify our inward poverty, God will give us the inner riches to overcome our outer struggle. We must spend time in God's Word and offer up our incense daily, both morning and evening. Then we can see God turn hate into love, disrespect into courtesy, dishonor and ill will into compassion, and judgment into mercy. These are inner riches that are available to us in Christ Jesus.

CHAPTER 17

Inspect

Morning also means to inspect. During my time in the military, we would have inspections often. It was just as common and routine as anything else we did, although not as often as other assigned military duties. Inspections helped us to maintain a certain level of readiness in fulfilling the job we were trained to do. The commanding generals (CG) inspection was the most daunting and exasperating of them all. We would routinely clean the same things over and over and over again, until the day of the inspection, making sure boots were shined, uniforms ironed, and hung neatly. Beds had to be made a certain way with a specific angle folded at the rear corners, and t-shirts and undergarments had to have specific measurements in length and width. We had to know the answers to questions about jobs pertaining to our military occupational status also known as (MOS), just to name a few things on the list when standing a CG inspection.

The best thing about this list of how to prepare for a CG was passed down from former soldiers who had already stood CG inspections down through the years and knew exactly what needed to be done to pass a commanding general's inspection. And when the day of the inspection finally arrived, we were ready because we trusted in the pass down. There have been many saints to go on before us. If we will take heed to the examples they left us and trust in the pass down of what to do and what not to do, we will be prepared for the final inspection as overcomers in the rapture to meet the commanding general of heaven and earth, our Lord and Savior Jesus Christ.

I shall never forget a lesson we were taught many years ago on this very principle. Every morning before the priest could minister in the priest's office and offer sacrifices for the people, the priests first had to thoroughly inspect their appearance in the mirror at the laver, to see if there was something in their appearance that needed correcting. The mirror that the priest used to inspect themselves was donated to the tabernacle by the women. This was important to the women because they would use their looking glasses to keep up their appearance. In so many words, they were willing to give up their appearance and donate their looking glasses to the tabernacle. One of the biggest problems we struggle with in life is losing our appearance in the eyes of other people. We will run to the end of the highway for appearance's sake. The message conveyed to us was that Jesus, who was the creator of all things both visible and invisible and the king of heaven, gave up His appearance when He came to Earth and took on a body and was found in fashion as a man.

> *...and being found in fashion as a man, he humbled himself, and became obedient unto death, even the death of the cross. Philippians 2:8*

He will never again look the same as He did before He came to save the human race. Before He came to Earth, He didn't have any wounds in His hands or His feet from the nails, He didn't have wounds in His head from a crown of thorns, He didn't have any cut, bruises and lacerations in his back by a whip of cat-o-nine tails, and He didn't have a ruptured heart from a spear that pierced Him. Jesus was willing to give up His appearance for you and me and will never again look the same as He did before He came to Earth. And if we are going to follow the Lamb wherever He goes, then we too must lose our appearance. As one song says, "When I learned how to lose, I found out how to win. I lost it all, to find everything."

It is amazing the extent we are willing to go just to save our appearance because we don't want to be associated with the wounds that God is allowing. We don't want the wounds because it changes who we are in the eyes of other people. We fear that people won't hold us in the same regard as before if we accept the wounds. And that may be true but the wounds are the only way we can know the fellowship of His suffering and be made conformable to his death. So we have to decide on whose appearance we are going to lose, either His or ours. We don't mind knowing the power of His resurrection because that isn't costing us anything; there are no wounds in that. But the fellowship of His suffering is costly and it requires that we embrace the wounds and give up our appearance, even if it means that we will never be the same in the eyes of some people who may at one time have held us in reputation.

God will allow others to see our flaws from the mistakes we made. He allows wounds of accusations and failures to separate us from some people that He knew we would not have separated from any other way. So now they no longer want to be identified with us because the wounds have changed their perception of us. God is the one who selects the people to who He wants to change our appearance when He sees the need for us to separate from them. And because of the wounds, our friendships and relationships will never be the same again.

The apostle Paul is by most accounts considered the greatest apostle and that is because he suffered the most and the more he suffered, the sweeter the incense of his relationship with Jesus was. The more suffering he endured for Christ's sake, the more he was conformed unto his death and the greater the odor of his incense spread abroad. Many people of his day inhaled the fragrance of the incense of his relationship with Christ and became followers of Christ. The power of his relationship was in the fragrance of the incense of his lifetime love and devotion to Jesus Christ. Long after his death, his relationship with Christ is still alive. The fragrance of that relationship was so powerful and so awesome that almost two thousand years later, people are still being drawn to Christ because of his commitment and sacrifice of service. By offering himself upon the altar he became "an odor of a sweet smell, a sacrifice acceptable and well pleasing to God" (Phil. 4:18).

We too have the same opportunity as did the apostle Paul to offer ourselves on the altar and long after we are gone, the fragrance of our relationship can still touch the lives of others. We should always be mindful that we are not just serving this present generation but we are serving generations to come, to leave behind a fragrance that transcends the days of our earthly journey. When they are assailed by the testing and trials of this life, there will be a sweet fragrance they can inhale that will testify to them that they too can overcome because we overcame and have left behind an overcoming fragrance of enduring hope. We will be known of all men by the odor we leave behind in the circumstances of life. So let the sweet fragrance of our relationship with the Lord Jesus Christ still be alive long after we have finished our course on Earth and our journey in time has expired.

CHAPTER 18

Making Mentions of You

Everyone wants to be loved, accepted, and included. It is human nature for us to have a longing for acceptance and to hear that someone has been thinking of us and praying for us. Making mentions of one another in prayer is how we can all be brought to the throne of Grace. Someone was mindful of us and included us in their prayers to God.

> *Grace be unto you, and peace, from God our Father and the Lord Jesus Christ. We give thanks to God for you always for you all, making mentions of you in our prayers.* 1 Thessalonians 1:1-2

Just as the heart is an organ that pumps blood throughout the body via the circulatory system, supplying oxygen and nutrients to the tissues and removing carbon dioxide and other wastes, prayer is the heart of our spiritual existence. It allows the supernatural blood of Jesus Christ to supply oxygen and nutrients to the other body organs. We live by each other prayers, as well as our own. The oxygen your prayer will supply for me and the rest of the body is vital for the continued existence and effectual working in the body of Christ. When the rest of the body of Christ becomes as important to us as our local assembly and when the needs of other saints are as important as our own needs, then God will be able to trust us to pump oxygen into other parts of the body of Christ. He'll do this by placing on us special burdens that may not be connected to anyone we know. Or he'll place a burden upon us to help supply for needs that don't have our name on them.

I remember an experience God gave me seven years ago. He would wake me up at midnight every night for ten days. And I would go to my prayer closet and weep uncontrollably for two hours straight and it would stop at 2 a.m. every morning. But while I was praying, I could feel the hurt and pain of all different kinds of people and all the different types of circumstances of the life they were subjected to. I could feel the hurt and pain of a child that was abused and unloved and not wanted by his parents. That was the hardest one for me to deal with. I could feel the pain of a faithful wife or a husband who had been hurt by an unfaithful spouse. I could feel the pain of a child being bullied and rejected by his peers.

I could feel the pain of men who longed to have a relationship with a father who never showed up in their lives or a little girl who wanted that kind of relationship with her mother but was rejected by the one who was supposed to love her. I could feel the pains of those who had been raped and molested and didn't know who to tell because sometimes the perpetrators would be someone close to them. I could feel the pain of those who experienced abnormal births or were born with some sort of disease and that made them look and feel like a misfit in life. You name it; I felt it for ten days. I could always tell what the spirit was praying for because the pain I felt and the tears I cried were specific to the circumstances the individuals were experiencing. There are a specific amount of tears that go along with that pain.

Mary K. Baxter talked about a specific occasion in her book on a *Divine Revelation of Heaven*. On one occasion, an angel escorted her during her out-of-body experience in heaven to the tear room where all the tears of the saints were kept. And the angel took a tear from a bottle that a woman had cried from a painful situation she went through. And he dropped one tear on a sheet of paper and the tear wrote down all the pain she suffered in that particular situation.

While I was praying, I somehow knew and was made aware that there was a place in God where everyone would be safe and they would not be hurting anymore. I didn't know where that place was, but I became aware that such a place existed. So I wept and I cried for God to take these people whose burdens I was feeling to that special place in Him so they would no longer feel hurt and pain. I believe God allowed me to share His broken heart for different people and how sin has so painfully marred the human race. I can remembered for a while after that experience, at work, and home, I was nothing but a big ball of water. Even when the experience was over, the effect that it had on me would stay with me for about another two weeks. I would spend my lunch breaks at work taking a walk because the fountains of my head were open from those experiences I had from midnight to 2 a.m.

This is the reason why we need to stay in a relationship with God because someone needs oxygen and God may want to use you and me to send it to that part of the body. We won't know it until eternity when He makes it known just how many people kept the faith and held on in difficult times because we were willing vessels making mention of them in prayer through the Spirit, without knowledge of what their circumstances were or even who they were. We must maintain an unbiased approach to prayer and just be a vessel to allow God to send spiritual oxygen wherever it is needed in His body. God will use those who make themselves available to Him. So as we make mention of the saints of God in our prayers we are allowing the blood of Christ to flow freely to the needs of His spiritual body. I choose to continue to make myself available, to give myself to be used by God on your behalf because "You are important to me and I need you to survive"

CHAPTER 19

The Circle of Unity

There is a common belief of untruth being told and accepted by some Christians concerning the origin of the circle. And I want to use this segment to refute, reject and debunk that myth. We should reject the notion that the circle has its origin in witchcraft. The devil doesn't have anything except what he stole from God and corrupted it for his prideful gain. All it takes for a lie to spread is not enough Christians standing up and pushing back against the false narratives. My spiritual mother, the late Reverend B. R. Hicks was an amazing woman of God. One thing I can recall from her personal testimony is that she said early in her walk with the Lord as a newborn Christian, one of the first lessons the Lord taught her was to hold on to every block of truth He gives her. The reason why, is the devil will try to talk you out of it and if He succeeds in talking you out of one block, He will talk you out of another block and keep pushing you back until He talks you out of your very salvation.

I want to spend this segment confirming and defending the truth that the circle belongs to God and the unity of the brotherhood. From the very beginning of our life, it has been in our nature to do things in the form of a circle. We make circles in the family altar, in Christian fellowship, when we huddle in football, in basketball, and in just about every sport world-wide they huddle in a circle. Even the Jews danced in circles during the feasts of Israel and at their weddings. We gathered into circles without thinking about it because part of our very being is in a circular pattern.

> *The tongue is a fire, a world of iniquity: so is the tongue among our members, that it defileth the whole body, and setteth on fire the COURSE of nature. James 3:6*

The word for course means a wheel. A wheel is round and has the resemblance of a circle. This is how God fashioned us on the inside. We know that our tongue cannot ignite a literal fire, so the apostle James must be talking about something on the inside of us. The course of nature is the same as saying the wheel of nature.

> *I will praise thee, for I am fearfully and wonderfully made: marvelous are thy works; and that my soul knoweth right well. Psalm 139:14*

Part of the way God made us is like a wheel which is the identical form of a circle. To become more enlightened on this subject I recommend that you read the book by Reverend B. R. Hicks called *Man's Threefold Nature.* Not only is the wheel of our nature round like a circle but the same God who created us also created the earth round just like a circle.

> *To whom then will ye liken God? Or what likeness will ye compare unto him? ...It is he that sitteth upon the circle of the earth, and the inhabitants thereof are as grasshoppers; that stretcheth out the heavens as a curtain, and spreadeth them out as a tent to dwell in. Isaiah 40:18, 22*

According to the Word of God, the earth is made like a circle. Are you trying to tell me that witchcraft was around when God first created the earth before any life existed on the earth? If not, then how is it possible that the circle belongs to witchcraft? The circle belongs to the unity of the brotherhood.

After Moses, the servant of the Lord died and Joshua had been given a charge by God to take Israel across the Jordan, they came to a place where God commanded Joshua to circumcise the males of the children of Israel that were born in the wilderness. And they called the name of that place Gilgal, which ironically means a wheel or a circle. So here again we see God operating in the circle. Jesus was from a small city called Nazareth, which happens to be a part of Galilee. The word Galilee means a circle. After Jesus was raised from the dead, He told the women to tell His disciples to meet Him in Galilee.

> *Then said Jesus unto them, Be not afraid: go tell my brethren that they go into Galilee, and there shall they see me. Matthew 28:10*

Jesus wanted to meet His disciples in the circle of the brotherhood and that is why He commanded them to meet Him in Galilee or the circle. Do you think that Jesus would have told His disciples to meet Him in the circle if the circle belonged to witchcraft? Or do you think that Jesus and His disciples were involved in witchcraft? Absolutely not! Witchcraft belongs to the powers of darkness and Jesus conquered all of the powers of darkness when He arose from the dead. This is how you can know that the circle belongs to God and not to witches and warlocks. They stole the circle to practice unity against God and His people. There's always the essential nature of extrinsic forces uniting together to come against the brotherhood of the Lord Jesus Christ. There are no enemies in the circle of the brotherhood. The twenty-four elders in the book of Revelation were situated round about the throne of Him that sat thereon.

> *And he that sat was to look upon like a jasper and a sardine stone: and there was a rainbow round about the throne, in sight like unto an emerald. And round about the throne were four and twenty seats: and upon the seats I saw four and twenty elders sitting, clothed in white raiment; and they had on their heads crowns of gold. Revelation 4:3-4*

This is a scene in heaven where a door was opened and the apostle John is describing what he saw. The meaning of the word *roundabout* is a *circle*. There was a rainbow roundabout and twenty-four elders were sitting in a circle round about the throne. Now, do you believe that God is going to allow witches to sit around His throne? As I said before, all it takes for the devil to change the truth into a lie is for enough Christians to observe wrong and not do anything about it. Even Winston Churchill said, "Truth is incontrovertible, ignorance can deride it, panic may resent it, malice may destroy it, but in the end there it is it will stand up again."

What I'm saying is true. And what people hate the most is when you speak the truth directly to the error inside of them. We are not true representatives of right until we can call out the wrong in ourselves just as loud as we can call it out in someone else. To become true examples of the brotherhood we must be willing to do everything within our power to endeavor to keep the unity of the brotherhood of the Lord Jesus Christ. We have come to the place where people are willing to openly change the truth for a lie, and the only reality they want to know is the one where they control the narrative. And when that happens, they can call the truth anything they want it to be.

This know also, that in the last days perilous times shall come. For men shall be lovers of their own selves, covetous, boasters, proud, blasphemers, disobedient to parents, unthankful, unholy, Without natural affection, trucebreakers, false accusers, incontinent, fierce, despisers of those that are good, Traitors, heady, high-minded, lovers of pleasures more than lovers of God; Having a form of godliness, but denying the power thereof: from such turn away. 2 Timothy 3:1-5

This is the condition of the world we are living in, and it is called the last days. The last days means the end of days. These are the true signs of the time and it should provoke something in us to get real with God regardless of who and what we have to turn loose to make it happen.

We cannot allow the circle to be taken away from the Christian culture, so stand up and take back the circle of unity of the brotherhood. The circle belonged to us long before witchcraft started using it. There is power in unity and our adversary knows it and this is why he is trying so subtly to convince unlearned Christians that the circle belongs to him, instead of them. Remember, he is the father of lies and he will employ whatever means necessary to steal the truth from your heart. You cannot be passive in this matter because if we let the devil come in and take the circle from us then the unity of the brotherhood will be defeated and then he can take anything he wants after that. This is one of those situations where we have to rise, get violent, and take it by force.

And from the days of John the Baptist until now the kingdom of heaven suffereth violence and the violent take it by force. Matthew 11:12

The time has come for the true brotherhood to risk everything to keep the unity of Spirit in the bond of peace. Do not let those who still want to embrace the lie that the circle belongs to witchcraft push you one inch backward. Do not accept the lie regardless of who it is that is selling the myth. Don't let them impose their falsehood on you just because they have a title. There is more proof in the scriptures about the origin of the circle, but I believe I have given you enough to take back the circle with confidence and love for the brethren...

CHAPTER 20

The Brand and the Name

Every owner recognizes that when a company is in its startup phase and they want to sell their product to the masses they have to first prove the value of the brand because no one knows the product by name. So in the beginning the brand has to sell the name before the name can sell the brand. The more the brand becomes a proving commodity and people see the quality of the brand the order will eventually switch, and the name will sell the brand.

> *Now when he was in Jerusalem at the feast of the Passover, many believed in his name, when they saw the miracles which he did. John 2:23*

Jesus carried the brand of the Godhead in His relationship with His heavenly Father. No one would have accepted Jesus as the only legitimate Son of God until they saw the pure nature of the brand. Jesus had to prove by deeds that He was the Son of God or His name would not have had any effect. He had to first prove the character and quality of the brand and the pure loving and forgiving nature of the Father before anyone would accept the name. But once He proved the validity and the authenticity of the brand the name of Jesus sold the brand of the Father. We can't sell people on the name of Christian until our lifestyle and conduct represent the brand of what a Christian should be.

When the brand of your relationship has lost its savior, people don't want to hear about Jesus if all you have to offer them is just a name. Without the lifestyle to represents who Jesus is, you become the cross's worst rival. You cannot be a Christian in name only because if you don't possess the brand you will misrepresent the name. You have to be branded in the way you live because people will buy that before they buy any name. Once they see the quality and character of your relationship with Jesus, the name will sell the brand. The brand is nothing more than the relationship you have with Jesus Christ. The church has lost its brand by allowing the world to come into the church and dictate its ideology of how the church is supposed to run, how we are supposed to worship, and what we can and cannot preach without offending them for one reason or another.

The world's footprints are getting bigger in the church and the church's footprints are getting smaller in the world. When the world's influence in the church is greater than the church's influence on the world this is a true sign of how lukewarm the church of God has become. When pastors are allowing their members to play and dance to different kinds of worldly music in the house of God, is not this the sign of a backslidden lukewarm church age? Spiritually speaking we are in the darkest part of the church age called Laodicea which is right before the rapture. And spiritual darkness will increase which is when the love of many will grow cold and many of the saints will lose spiritual strength and desire, to continue to fight a good fight. We must resolve to find refuge in offering our incense morning and evening, and there in the secret place we will find the strength to press on.

The principles of holiness and separation are just as good today as they were in the days of the apostles; it's just that many Christians are no longer embracing them as they embraced them in those days. As Christians, we don't have the influence that we once had because we went away from the principles of who we once were. I once heard a preacher give an altar call and tell the people that they don't have to stop doing anything they are doing because God will meet them right where they are. When he said that, I thought to myself, he just defeated the purpose for the altar call. I didn't have any problem with God meeting them where they are, my problem was telling them to keep sinning and not make any effort to give the grace of God a chance to work. "Shall we sin, that grace may abound? God forbid." That is not how you start a new Christian out on their journey. What about discipleship? I heard a poet from passion for Christ movement (p4cm) do a piece called "A lesson before dying" he made a profound statement that **"Jesus can not live in the same sins he died for".**

Another problem that hurts the body of Christ is that everybody wants to be right. Every argument, dispute, and disagreement is all about proving one right and the other wrong. And being right is neither the objective nor the focus of our calling. When Jesus stood in the judgment hall alone with those who condemned Him to death, never once did He engage with them about who was right and who was wrong. He was the King of Righteousness, the King of Right. To do His Father's will, which was to unify humanity with the Godhead was His goal and objective, so He refrained from the lesser argument of right to win the greater battle for unity. Jesus had a much greater vision and focus than just being right.

As a Christian brotherhood that represents Christ on Earth, we must refocus and rediscover the vision and come into alignment with it by a commitment to the fundamental principles that unite us and the blessed tie that binds us. It should always be our desire to represent the brand of what a Christian is supposed to be, to bring back respect and honor to the name of Jesus Christ. Then the unity of the brotherhood will become a fruitful bough whose branches run over the walls of denominations. We must decide what we want our bottom line to be, are we going to fight to be right or will we endeavor to keep the unity of the Spirit in the bond of peace. Sometimes we have to sacrifice the right for the greater prize of unity. Now, this doesn't apply to situations where you compromise your faith in Christ Jesus and in the moral principles of truth and sound doctrine in the slightest way just to satisfy the world. We must remember that we have been set for both the defense and confirmation of the gospel of Jesus Christ. But I'm talking to Christians everywhere who embrace the same fundamental belief in our Lord and Savior Jesus Christ.

This principle will work in all relationships, be it husband and wife, parent and children, sisters and brothers, if you have unity as a greater vision and focus than just being right, then humble yourself and give someone else the right, while you embrace the unity. The church age is almost over and if there is a chance for the survival of the brotherhood, we must be willing to give up our right for the greater good of unity among the brethren.

> *Behold how good and how pleasant it is for brethren to dwell together in unity. Psalm 133:1*

The good and pleasantness belong to all the brethren who are willing to give up their right for unity. The devil knows the power in unity and that is exactly why he is always influencing Christians to fight for right. When this kind of behavior persists in the body of Christ, it is like sending the body into a condition called autoimmune. The immune system attacks the body where it is normally designed to help fight bacteria, viruses, and foreign invaders, and to recognize and neutralize harmful substances from the environment by sending out an army of cells to fight against all invaders. But in autoimmune the cells that are supposed to be fighting for you begin to fight against you, and because of that, the body is at war with itself. This is a very sad description of how the body of Christ treats each other. Instead of us fighting for each other, we are warring against each other, because we prefer being right over being in unity, and when we do that, we neither represent the name nor the brand of the Godhead. This may not apply to all, but if one part of the body is sick, the whole body is sick. So we pray that our unity will one day be restored.

CHAPTER 21

The Genesis and the Exodus of Time

There is a Genesis and an Exodus to all the events that happen on the stage of time. Time is just like a big house that has a front door and a back door, with many rooms in between to display the events that have been ordained by God. Every person who has ever been born had to come through the front door except for our fore-parents Adam and Eve. They were the only exception to the rule. The front door of time is through the womb of our mother. There never will be a debate on this issue, since the entire human race had to follow the same protocol. Even our Lord Jesus Christ had to enter into the house of time through the front door.

And as we move through the stages of life from infancy to toddler, to early childhood, to adolescence, to early adulthood, to middle age, to late adulthood, there is one silver lining that connects all stages of growth and development, and that is the arrow keeps pointing toward the back door. We are not allowed to exit the same way we came in. Wasn't that the question Nicodemus asked Jesus, when Jesus told him, "You must be born again?" John.3:3. Nicodemus wanted to know how a man can enter again through the same door he came in. Jesus said, "That which is born of flesh is flesh, and that which is born of Spirit is Spirit." Nicodemus wasn't aware that Jesus was talking about an eternal birth, not temporal. In all of our encounters in life, the arrow still points to the back door. We are not allowed to return to the genesis of our earthly journey because the stage has been set for the exodus.

Jesus came through the front door of time through the womb of the Virgin Mary and after thirty-three and a half years, He left through the back door of the house of time. Although Jesus left out of the back door of time, He conquered death, hell, and the grave and took the keys, so that His followers will have immediate access into His kingdom upon their exodus from time. There are many different ways we can make our exodus from time although the cross may not be one of them. Whichever way God chooses for us will be the sufficient route. And just as He raised His Son, He will also raise those who have believed in Him.

> *And so it was, that, while they were there, the days were accomplished that she should be delivered. Luke 2:6*

There are an accomplished number of days before God delivers us to time, from our mother's womb, and there are also an accomplished number of days when we are delivered from time back into eternity. Both deliverances are necessary and are appointed by God. All the circumstances that God has appointed for us in time have a specific number of days to be accomplished for Him to work His purpose in us to bring to birth a new formation of the character and nature of Jesus Christ through us, and to the world around us. After the days have been accomplished for us to be delivered from time, we must prepare for the exodus.

CHAPTER 22

The Texture of Darkness

Evening means to cover over with a texture. Darkness is a texture that covers over whatever it comes in contact with. *Texture means the feel, the appearance, the consistency of a surface or substance.* When the texture of darkness begins to move over the heart it is ever so subtle, because it integrates truth with error before the effects of it are known. Most people are controlled by feelings and Christians are not exempt. If they don't feel a strong presence of the Spirit of God, they will not make the extra push to engage the Lord's presence for worship and fellowship. So as the texture of spiritual darkness begins to move over the heart it changes the inward appearance before it changes the outward appearance. Once our inward appearance is changed, the outward change will be reflected in the choices we make. Our actions are who we are. And once who we are changes, the things we do, the places we go, and the circle of people we hang with will change as well.

This is how the devil works, through a texture of darkness. You may have heard someone try to defend the actions of another person by saying, that's not who they are. I have been guilty of saying it. Jesus said that nothing can come out of a man except what is on the inside of him. It is necessary to stop running from the inherited sinful nature of Adam, the first, and start acknowledging these things for what they are and ask God to cleanse us from these evil things. All of the different sinful emotions that are played out of us are the part of us that belongs to the fallen inherited nature. So confess it and repent of it.

You might ask how you can know when you are being covered over with a texture of darkness. Your choices will gradually change and your desires will not be the same. The times when you would spend with God in prayer will be replaced with some other activity. Your desire for studying the Word of God will be swallowed up with a desire to have something else. You will begin to desire fellowship outside of the circle of Christianity, and the influence of that kind of fellowship will become your new normal. Everything will take a gradual turn away from God. When the things of God no longer interest you anymore, then the very things you once enjoyed doing and the people you enjoyed being around will begin to feel like strangers instead of your friends. Everything changes, because that's the nature and personality of the texture of darkness, which is to make subtle changes while giving the appearance that everything is still the same. Was this not the problem with the saints in Laodicea?

> *I am rich, increased with goods, and have need of nothing; and knowest not that thou art wretched, and miserable, and poor, and blind, and naked. Revelation 3:17*

The darkness had covered them with so much spiritual blindness that they were not able to see that they had been stripped naked in their relationship with Jesus Christ. The subtle changes that had been made changed their whole appearance before God. While they were proclaiming to be one thing, God saw them as being opposite. This is what is happening to the saints of our time. The apostle John received the revelation of the seven churches on the isle of Patmos. The seven churches had to do with the different church ages that the church would go through, with Laodicea being the last and darkest before the coming of the Lord. So right before the coming of the Lord, we find ourselves in the darkest part of the church age and the love of many is waxing cold because they have been covered with a texture of darkness and have become victims of the lukewarm environment of Laodicea.

Beware of a new wave of backsliders coming from among the Christian faith and boldly declaring that they have renounced the faith as if the validity and the authenticity of our faith depend upon their acceptance or rejection of it. It doesn't, it is firmly rooted and grounded in sacrificial death, burial, and resurrection of Jesus Christ, our Lord. They want to give the appearance that there is something better out there than Christianity. Although I disagree with it, I do however agree that we as a whole have not proved them wrong by our actions. I am aware that many sincere saints and leaders do it the right way and represent Christ well and wear the Christian badge with honor. But as a body we have to include everyone, even those who have given the world a reason to speak reproachfully about our Savior, bringing shame and embarrassment on the name of Jesus. And without being so quick to judge them, let us look at the times when we have been just as guilty for some of the same infractions, just in a different way and at a different time.

We have taken away the sweet fragrance from the name of Jesus and the world can no longer smell it and now Jesus is just another name to them. Our Savior has had too many facelifts and makeovers in the eyes of the world because it seems that some parts of the Christian culture are contending for the prize to be the next *American Idol* instead of preparing for the rapture. This is a texture of darkness that has subtly changed and challenged the solidarity of the basic principle of what we believe.

To avoid being overcome by a texture of darkness, we must reconnect with the vibrancy of our first love to prevent the effervescence of that relationship from dissolving into a lukewarm community of thoughts, feelings, and actions. We need to clean up what we have messed up before the eyes of God and relaunch the fundamental principles of our faith and the doctrine of what we believed until our walk with Christ has a more honorable and compelling influence than our talk.

CHAPTER 23

To Be Darkened

Finally, *evening* also means *to be darkened* which means *to be covered with darkness*. Some people have wrapped themselves so tightly in garments of darkness that they reject every ray of light that attempts to shine through. Anything that points them to their sinful condition they counter with some kind of rebuttal. They take the light that was meant to shine on them and divert it to someone else because they don't want the exposure the light brings to correct their way of living and to assume the responsibility to change. Jesus said that, "light has come into the world and men love darkness rather than light." John.3:19

In the previous chapter of this book, we briefly made mention of the letters written to the seven churches in Asia which represent the different periods the church will go through under the dispensation of grace. This was made effective through the new covenant after the death, burial, and resurrection of the Lord Jesus Christ. As the spiritual church age-progressed from one angel to another the light of the gospel began to fade and reached what is called the dark ages during the time of Thyatira, Pergamum, and Sardis. But the light of the gospel began to shine once again through the early reformers of the faith in the western civilization and in the Philadelphia church age, God once again raised up the light of the candlestick. The light of the gospel was once again burning brightly and there was a spiritual awakening with revival happening in many places in western civilization and beyond.

But through the process of time, a covering of darkness has set upon Christianity so subtly it has to a large degree, gone unrecognized within the Christian culture. That is how we arrived at the final church age called Laodicea, the darkest of all the previous church ages. This is that Laodicean Church Age that you and I are now living in, represented by the seventh and final angel. Seven is the number of completion. The lingering deception is that they thought they had it all, but were unaware that they had been influenced and captured by the personality of the age, which was lukewarmness. This was the condition of the church right before the rapture.

> *Because thou sayest, I am rich, and increased with goods, and have need of nothing; and knowest not that thou art wretched, and miserable, and poor and blind, and naked. Revelation 3:17*

> *Behold, I stand at the door and knock: if any man hear my voice, and open the door, I will come into him, and sup with him, and he with me. Revelation 3:20*

The Laodiceans were Christians, so why was Jesus knocking on the door of the hearts of Christians that He was supposed to already have access to, except they were backslidden and had allowed so much of the world to occupy the space and time that they once had given to Him? It's because they locked Him out of the door of their first love relationship. He was knocking because He knew that their preparation for the rapture depended on Him having access to the door of their first love. The times had diminished when they sought after God, spent time in the Word of God, waited on Him in prayer, and were glad when it was time to go to the house of the Lord. Times were fewer when they sang songs of praise and worship with the saints of God and joyfully heard the Word of God. Now they have taken on the personality of the church age and have been deceived into thinking that all of that is no longer necessary to be ready for the rapture. When we are content with excuses for letting other things occupy the time and space that once belonged to our first love relationship, it is only because our understanding has been darkened through compromise.

I believe that revival and the great awakening for the most part have already come to the church and now there will be a falling away first. That doesn't mean that others won't be saved and be added to the church. But I believe the next great awakening will be when the rapture takes place and Christians who played around will suddenly realize that they have missed it.

> *Let no man deceive you by any means: for that day shall not come, except there come a falling away first, and that man of sin be revealed, the son of perdition. 2 Thessalonians 2:3*

> *And because iniquity shall abound, the love of many shall wax cold. Matthew 24:12*

This talk about revival and spiritual awakening sweeping across the land does not coincide with the signs of the time. Jesus spoke of the signs of the end and there are two noticeable signs that He spoke of that are becoming more obvious with every passing moment. First, He said in Matthew 24: 37,

> *As it was in the days of Noah, so shall it be in the days of the coming of the Son of Man.*

How was it in the days of Noah? Only Noah found grace in the sight of the Lord. Mankind was so violent and filled with violence and hatred, murders, and injustice that God could no longer be a spectator of the violent events that were happening in every place on the earth where human life existed. So He was forced to remove and evict the tenants of the earth because they disrupted the ebb and flow of the kind of relationship God wanted to have between heaven and Earth.

> *The earth also was corrupt before God, and the earth was filled with violence....And God said unto Noah, The end of all flesh is come before me; for the earth is filled with violence through them; and, behold, I will destroy them with the earth. Genesis 8:11, 13*

> *Like also as it was in the days of Lot...Even thus shall it be in the day when the Son of man is revealed. Luke 17:28, 30*

How was it in the days of Lot? Adultery, fornication, and idolatry which include all sorts of immoral behaviors were on display in those days. Men had become corrupt in their desire and craved for an experience with the same gender, men with men and women with women, which violated the principle of the marriage union between a male and female. Moreover, it violated the principle to be fruitful and multiply which can only happen in a union that God Himself established from the beginning between a male and a female of every living species that dwell upon the earth, that lives in the water, and that fly in the firmament. Yet, mankind who God gave dominion over all things has become the only living creature that is violating the principle, to be fruitful and multiply. Adultery breaks the marriage union and weakens the family tree and its ability to function properly.

All versions of sexual sins, idolatry, indecency and injustice played a role in the overthrow of Sodom and Gomorrah.

> *And changed the glory of an uncorruptible God into an image made like unto corruptible man, into birds, into four footed beasts, and creeping things. Wherefore God gave them up to uncleanness through the lust of their own hearts, to dishonour their own bodies between themselves. Who changed the truth of God into a lie, and served the creature more than the Creator, who is blessed forever Amen. For this cause God gave them up unto vile affections: for even their women did change the natural use into that which is against nature: And likewise also the men, leaving the natural use of the woman, burned; men with men working that which is unseemly, and receiving in themselves that recompense of their error which was meet. And even as they did not like to retain God in their knowledge, God gave them over to a reprobate mind, to do those things which are not convenient. Romans 1:23-28*

These are all the signs of the end of time, and it is happening just like Jesus said it would. As much as we may hope for revival and great awakening, the events of our time are very consistent with the explanation of scriptures and how it is supposed to be before the coming of the Lord. It is now time to rise to a new awakening inside of yourself and see if Jesus is first place in your desire or have you replaced Him with something or someone else. If you have, it isn't too late to let Him back in.

You have to first understand that we do not have to leave home to be a prodigal son or daughter. It's not where we go physically that makes the journey a far country. It is how far we go when we stray from our relationship with Jesus Christ and embrace behaviors and lifestyles that we know

God is not pleased with. And although we may have not left home physically, we can go on a long journey of sinful living until God brings us to a place of repentance and a new desire to return to the Father's house. You have to go to a place within yourself called the *honesty room* and measure the choices and actions that you are making now with the ones you made when Jesus was your main attraction.

Unprincipled behavior is beginning to take control of the premise of religious freedom and its moral foundation. The Christian culture is in a moral freefall. We can't live by a double standard and expect God to bless us. When we sin, there is the automatic condemnation that goes along with the sin. God's condemnation is upon every sinful action regardless of what it is and who is doing it. His judgments show no respect for a person or position. If the church continues to be actively involved in giving a free pass to immoral behavior with a platform of equal rights to stand on, we may not ever recover from the poison of this kind of serpent's bite.

We must stop giving unprincipled mentalities a voice of reason in our churches; this is nothing but a covering of darkness that has descended upon Christianity. When the church becomes silent on moral issues, their silence will become their loudest cry of regret. Where immoral conduct is accepted in its beginning stages, it will continue to spread its wings until it has gained complete acceptance as part of the norm. Then they will no longer request, but demand they have it their way. The reason why the moral principles continue to erode is that the church has become hypnotized through compromise.

It must have been about four years ago that I was grieving or maybe complaining to the Lord over all the violence and rage that had begun to become a normal occurrence in our nation. I was asking God, "Why are you allowing this to happen?" And the Spirit of God spoke to me and said, "This is just a mist of what's getting ready to happen on planet earth."

He reminded me of the days of Noah. Some Hebrew scholars assert and believe that although it did not rain before the flood, the dark clouds were gathering and the closer they got to the time of the flood, they began to feel a mist falling on them from above as a warning to them that something was getting ready to happen. They were only aware of a mist that came up to water the ground; never before had they experienced a mist falling on them.

Could it be that in His mercy and long-suffering not willing that any should perish, God sent a mist from above as a last result to get their attention? But they did not take it to heart and would soon find out that the mist was the final warning before the flood. Jesus said, "Before the flood they were eating and drinking, marrying and giving in marriage, until the day that Noah entered into the ark." Matt.24:38 This is important because you need to be careful whose doctrine and teachings you are eating and drinking. It will either get you into the ark or it is going to keep you out of it.

The dark clouds of the spiritual night season are gathering in and are an indication that the floods of ungodly men are getting ready to take over the world. So what we are seeing right now with the violence and the killings is just a mist of what is getting ready to happen during the Tribulation Period after the Rapture has taken place. Only the saints who have prepared and made themselves ready will be counted worthy to escape all those things that shall come upon the earth and participate in that glorious event that will soon be upon us. Don't be overcome by the darkness of this spiritual night season. We are all in it together just before the coming of the Lord.

> *Wherefore gird up the loins of your mind, be sober, and hope to the end for the grace that is be brought unto you at the revelation of Jesus Christ. 1 Peter 1:13*

In expressing my final thoughts to you, it is my earnest and deepest desire that you will understand all the more both the purpose and the necessity to begin a faithful journey of offering up your morning and evening sacrifice. Let your incense rise in worship to establish an ongoing relationship with the Lord Jesus Christ. Don't do it part-time, do it at all times. There is insecurity inside of us that doesn't believe His grace is sufficient to work this kind of obedience within us. I am a living witness that He can and will do it. If He did it for me, He will do it for you. There will be times when you won't feel like offering up your incense in the morning or evening. Do not let how you feel stop you from spending time alone with God in prayer. Make yourself do anyway because your eternal destiny depends on it. Start applying discipline to yourself until spending time in God's presence becomes a habit. It is possible to establish good spiritual habits.

John Maxwell said, "Discipline make habits your servant instead of your master."

Once we form the right habits they will serve us and help us do the right thing without thinking about how we feel. Forming good, morally clean, and wholesome habits means everything, especially in the day in which we live.

Zig Zigler said, "The chains of habit are so light to be felt, until they are too heavy to be broken."

Reverend B.R. Hicks said, "If you sow a habit you will reap a character and if you sow a character, you will reap a destiny."

Who ever heard of having a relationship with someone but never spending any time with them to approve and confirm the validity of the relationship? I have never heard of two people falling in love and not wanting to be in each other's presence. God measures our love for Him by the amount of time we are willing to spend in His presence; not His service, because service can be used as a substitute to avoid His presence sometimes.

What I mean by His presence is when you deliberately set aside some time in a secret meeting place with Him and Him alone; making every moment count for the things that He has done for you, in you, and through you.

If you are not offering up your incense to God morning or evening, He has no way of confirming and validating the relationship. The only confirmation He has is in the incense we offer. Our obedience to His Word and spending time in His presence are the qualifying components for being clothed in our spiritual garments and to hear the sound of the trumpet. We have come this far by faith, leaning on the Lord, trusting in His holy Word, He's never failed us yet and we can't turn around now, because we have come this far by faith" So *May Our Incense Rise*... until soon and very soon we will rise with it. There will be brighter days ahead in the eternal tomorrow. May God bless you always and forever, Amen.

CPSIA information can be obtained
at www.ICGtesting.com
Printed in the USA
LVHW082021080822
725450LV00013B/436

9 781662 850103